European Issues in Children's
Identity and Citizenship **4**

Social learning, inclusiveness and exclusiveness in Europe

Edited by Beata Krzywosz-Rynkiewicz and Alistair Ross

Children's
Identity &
Citizenship
in Europe

Trentham Books
Stoke on Trent, UK and Sterling USA

The publication of this volume has been supported by the Directorate
General for Education and Culture of the European Commission through the
Socrates programme

Trentham Books Limited

Westview House	22883 Quicksilver Drive
734 London Road	Sterling
Oakhill	VA 20166-2012
Stoke on Trent	USA
Staffordshire	
England ST4 5NP	

First published 2004

British Library Cataloguing-in-Publication Data
A catalogue record for this book is available from the British Library

ISBN 1 85856 326 7

Designed and typeset by Trentham Print Design Ltd., Chester and printed in Great Britain by Cromwell Press Ltd., Wiltshire.

Contents

v

Series Introduction:
European Issues in Children's
Identity and Citizenship

Social learning, inclusiveness and exclusiveness in Europe is the
fourth volume in the series European Issues in Children's Identity
and Citizenship. This collection has arisen from the work of the
ERASMUS Thematic Network Project called Children's Identity and
Citizenship in Europe (CiCe). This Network brings together over
90 University Departments, in 29 European states, all of whom
share an interest in the education of professionals who will work
with children and young people in the area of social, political and
economic education. The Network links many of those who are
educating the future teachers, youth workers, social pedagogues
and social psychologists in Europe.

The CiCe Network began in 1996, and has been supported by the
European Commission since 1998. It is now in a major second
phase of development, which will run to late 2005. This series
stems from our conviction that changes in contemporary European
society are such that we need to examine how the processes and
outcomes of socialisation are adapting to the new contexts.
Political, economic and social changes are underway that suggest
that we are developing multi-faceted and layered identities, that
reflect the contingencies of European integration. In particular,
children are growing up in this rapidly changing society, and their
social behaviour will reflect the dimensions of this new and
developing social unit. Identities will probably be rather different:
national identities will continue alongside new identifications, with
both sub-national regions and with supra-national unions. Our
sense of citizenship will also develop in rather different ways than
in the past: multiple and nested loyalties will develop, more complex than the simple affiliations of the past.

Those who will work with children and young people have a particular role to play in this. They will have to help young people develop their own relationships with the new institutions that develop, while at the same time being mindful of the traditional relationships known and understood by parents and grandparents, and their role in inter-generational acculturation.

This series is designed to discuss and debate the issues concerned with the professional and academic education of teachers, early childhood workers, social pedagogues and the like. They will need to understand the complex issues surrounding the socialisation and social understanding of the young, and to be aware of the similarities and differences in professional practices across Europe. They will need to work with young people learning to be citizens – citizens both of the traditional political entities, and of the developing new polities of Europe.

This fourth volume in the series has a focus on socialisation and social learning in the complexities of European societies that are engaged in rapid transformations. It is linked to and follows two earlier volumes, *Young People's Understanding of Economic Issues in the New Europe* (Hutchings, Fülop and Van den dries, 2002) and *Political Learning and Citizenship in Europe* (Roland-Lévy and Ross, 2003).

CiCe welcomes enquiries from potential members of the Network. These should be addressed to the CiCe Central Co-ordination Unit, at the Institute for Policy Studies in Education, London Metropolitan University, 166–220 Holloway Road, London N7 8DB, United Kingdom.

Alistair Ross

Series Editor

On behalf of the editorial committee: Tilman Allert, Marta Fülop, Akos Gocsal, Soren Hegstrup, Riitta Korhonen, Emilio Lastrucci, Elisabet Näsman, Panyota Papoulia-Tzelpi, Christine Roland-Lévy and Ann-Marie van Den Dries

Chapter Synopsis

Chapter One: Socialisation and learning about society in contemporary Europe

This chapter contextualises the four parts that follow. **Beata Krzywosz-Rynkiewicz** (Poland) and **Alistair Ross** (UK) set out the themes of socialisation and of social learning, arguing that these processes become more complex as European societies become more intricate and inter-linked. While initial socialisation may still, in some instances, take place in relatively homogeneous social contexts, the increasingly plural society that constitutes modern Europe requires the exercise of a greater degree of social understanding and tolerance. Social learning requires a level of meta-socialisation, in which critical analysis, tolerance, and a willingness to try and understand the perspectives of others are essential elements. They argue that the unfolding nature of the collection in this volume will contribute to an understanding of this: moving from the establishment of identity in a social context to the development of social relationships; and contrasting social learning at different stages of the educational system and examining the major triad of social distinction and exclusion: ethnicity, gender and class.

Part One: The formation of social identity

Chapter Two: The role of family in the formation of social identity

The significant elements of early socialisation are set out in the chapter by **Julia Spinthourakis** and **John Katsillis** (Greece). They argue that the composition and role of the family are changing very quickly, and extended family patterns of monocultural society have been replaced by nuclear or permeable family patterns, particularly so in Europe. Changes in family organisation lead to differentiated relationships that impact on the development of children's social identity: parenting is no longer simply the domain of traditional primary caregivers. New social values and skills are needed by children, and those responsible for their primary socialisation. They argue that the role of the family in the formation of children's social identity is critical, and to examine this role they outline social identity and examine the role of the family in this process and its influence on the formation of children's social identity.

Chapter Three: The role of school in acquiring social identity by children: searching for a new image of Polish education

Systematic and political changes in Poland have influenced all spheres of social life including education. We now view schooling as preparation for being active in social life. The main educational issues in this are the cultural variety of the world, questions about the development of social identity, perceptions of social difference in its widest meaning and open dialogue with 'the other'. In this chapter, **Marzenna Nowicka** (Poland) considers how the school as institution prepares children for interaction with 'the other'. After a presentation of modern trends of social education in Poland, she discusses formal dimensions of socialisation, including conscious-ness and the planning activities of teachers (selection of subject-matter, class and school customs). The chapter concludes with a consideration of informal and unplanned socialisation, including communication during lessons and contacts with peers beyond the didactic process.

Part Two: The development of social relationships

Chapter Four: 'Respect between teachers and students is the basis for all school work': Teacher-student relationships

In this chapter **Sigrún Adalbjarnardóttir** (Iceland) focuses on the key role teachers play in organising constructive and meaningful experiences for their students as they promote their students' social,

x

ethical, and intellectual growth while learning about society and social relationships. She advocates a social constructivist approach. On the one hand, this is with an emphasis on structural-developmental theories of how children and adolescents develop their understanding of social, ethical, and interpersonal issues. In particular, she examines children's and adolescents' perspective-taking ability – the developing ability to differentiate and coordinate different perspectives – as a base both for students' understanding of values and rules in societies, and for their skills in social relationships, such as in negotiating and coming to an agreement over conflicting interpersonal, social, and ethical issues. On the other hand, she analyses how teachers can foster this core capacity of perspective-taking, as a base for developing children's and adolescents' understanding of values and rules in societies, as well as their social skills. The chapter outlines teaching styles and teaching strategies that aim to promote students' understanding and skill in this area, noting how students learn both 'by' and 'about' social relationships, rules and values from social relationships between teachers and students. It concludes with a discussion of the importance of teacher professional awareness (pedagogical vision, aims, teaching strategies and styles) in relation to their students' social understanding and skills.

Chapter Five: The development of social relationship between students

This chapter, written by **Edgar Krull** and **Tiiu Kadajane** (Estonia), introduces and analyses issues of social relationships between pupils from the point of view firstly, of developmental changes in student social skills, and secondly, of teachers' opportunities for creating favourable conditions for these changes. To this end, research findings on these issues are surveyed and analysed. An educational focus requires the linking of knowledge of developmental changes to teachers' educational activities, and this leads to a third theme: uncovering social structures in pupil groups. Developmental changes in social skills are explored, as are the development of friendship structures and attitudes of mutual acceptance and respect between pupils. Several sociometrical approaches are introduced and analysed, which teachers might use as tools for uncovering social relationships between pupils in their classes. The third theme of this chapter is supporting the development of pupils' social skills, introducing and discussing different approaches to correcting irregular social relations between pupils.

Part Three: Social Education at different ages

Chapter Six: Early Childhood Education: a meeting place for challenges

Children begin pre-school as a first step in the early childhood education process. As **Ingrid Pramling Samuelsson** and **Anette Emilson** describe this in Sweden, it takes place between the ages of one and five years. Children enter a system built upon a mix of features from the home, the kindergarten and school. Furthermore, children also encounter their own personal experience of a collective arena with societal intentions. Challenges arise for further growth and learning at this crossroads between the single child and the group of children.

Chapter Seven: Who is afraid of social learning?

Hugo Verkest (Belgium) takes us in this chapter from early childhood education to primary education. Education in Belgium is a regional matter, and in Flanders social learning is encompassed in the new primary schools' curriculum area of 'world orientation'. The chapter examines how much this curriculum differs from earlier curricula, dating from 1936 and 1954. It describes the reluctant way in which the new syllabus is being implemented. Recent researchers describe the current context of social learning as turning bitter and becoming filled with a general malaise, particularly for those who get most of their information from commercial television stations. This media dominance also contributes to the lack of emphasis given to certain controversial themes such as food, security, human rights, waste, elections and racism. Why are adults so scared of this subject matter? What are they afraid of? Interviews and personal observations are used to highlight the factors that may counter this, such as emotional, ecological and visual factors, and how to integrate these in classroom and school contexts to establish trust during social learning.

Chapter Eight: Youth and society in France: between common conceptions and school knowledge

This chapter moves from the primary school to secondary education. Drawing from research with French teenagers, **Nicole Tutiaux-Guillon** and **Jane Mejias** examine how social topics are understood by French students between the ages of 13/14 and the final years of school (aged 17/18). A consistent picture of how young people understand social facts and society emerges around constructions of work, family, social change, social ties, rich/poor and the usual or 'right' course for a society. The chapter then links this knowledge to what students actually learn in school through the analysis of three cases: where student conceptions and teaching are consistent, where teaching passes on interpretations of social facts which students reshape to fit with their preconceptions, and where what is taught in school is taken on only for the purpose of formal school assessments but dismissed for 'real life' purposes.

Part Four: Issues in contemporary European society

Chapter Nine: National and ethnic prejudices and their origins

This chapter argues that prejudices are negative attitudes, that is, feelings of unfavorableness, and that negative attitudes facilitate negative behaviour. **Henk Dekker** (Netherlands) focuses on prejudices with respect to nationalities and ethnic minorities. He considers both specific negative attitudes, such as distrust, and general negative attitudes. Research shows low levels of trust among European nationalities, negative attitudes toward foreign European countries among a considerable proportion of the young in several European countries, and widespread ethnic exclusion. Negative attitudes, which originate from negative affective experiences such as direct contact, are derived from previously acquired negative perceptions such as stereotypes and clichés, and negative feelings, and are the effect of negative informative and emotional messages from relevant others. Background variables of national favouritism, feelings of national superiority and a sense of positive identity are considered. All these are related to educational interventions designed to reduce prejudices, including planned exchange programmes, interethnic cooperation projects, and the use of meta-stereotypes.

Chapter Ten: Gender(ed) issues in Citizenship Education

This chapter begins by introducing key relationships between gender and citizenship education, and raising questions about the transformation of schooling and the range of discourses in our globalised and complex society. **Florbela Trigos-Santos** (Portugal) goes on to problematise the progress toward gender equality and the effects of change on young people. She then considers theoretical frameworks: accounts of empirical and theoretical research range from main theoretical problems raised in the literature to new approaches in the study of gender and education. Gendered educational performance in contemporary schooling is discussed in terms of the current shift in educational achievement of boys and girls, and of the debate about similarity and difference in patterns of schooling. How can we explain girls' success? Are gendered relations patterns changing? Finally, this chapter asks how citizenship education should address gender for an equal participation in the educational process. The findings remain inconclusive: the debate on the implications for a democratic society goes on.

Chapter Eleven: Social class and educational opportunities

Developmental theories contrast the relative importance of heredity and the environment, but **Marjanca Pergar Kuščer** (Slovenia) argues that experiences and learning opportunities in the early years have greatest impact on future life. Socially deprived environments are key: there is much evidence that children from different social classes have vastly different educational achievements. The average higher social status child stays in school longer and does better while there then does the lower social status child. Social class may be influential in different ways: this chapter stresses teacher attitudes towards social class. Pupils who do not conform to middle-class norms risk being considered less good students, regardless of their ability. The feeling of success the child acquires in the first years of schooling is critical for their self-esteem. Respect and acceptance contributes to striving for better academic results, and leads to better relations with peers. The influence of the teacher can depend on their understanding of, and reaction to, the child's social class.

1

Introduction:
Socialisation and learning about
society in contemporary Europe

Beata Krzywosz-Rynkiewicz and Alistair Ross

This volume encompasses two aspects of social learning. The first is about the processes of socialisation, through which the individual comes to behave as a member of a social group – traditionally, through the primary socialisation of the family, followed by the secondary socialisation brought about by wider social institutions such as school, peers and society. The second aspect concerns meta-socialisation: consciously learning about how society works. This is a rather different kind of learning: it involves a knowing and deliberate appreciation of social structures, processes and patterns of behaviour. It is the development of an engagement with and thinking about how society ought to be, rather than simply participating in an established order. It involves understanding and critiquing social difference, and challenging practices of social exclusion, including racism, xenophobia, gender-based discrimination, and a range of other anti-inclusive practices – islamophobia, homophobia, prejudice against the disabled, and so on.

These two aspects are related, but they are distinct. The individual socialised in a particular narrow community may behave in anti-social ways if they become part of a larger and more diverse society. Resocialisation may follow. But learning about society at the meta-level requires more than simply re-learning behavioural patterns to deal with new kinds of difference. It involves the development and use of abstract concepts, the ability to question critically, skills of analysis, interpretation, and judgement of social interaction.

Children and young people learn about society in many ways, both informal and formal. Informal social learning has happened since the earliest societies: children observe patterns of social behaviour by the people around them, and then generalise and discern 'rules' that govern these, which they tend to both follow and test. The responses they get confirm them in their generalisations, or cause them to shift their definition to more accurately reflect all of their experiences. Formal social learning takes place in social institutions – the family as well as in schools – and has tended to be more instructional: the formal transmission of patterns or rules, rather than the social construction of informal learning. However, there are modern examples of teaching that uses social constructivist approaches in school settings. Schools may categorise certain social concepts as those that are important, and try to ensure that children come across diverse examples of these, that may help them generalise in an inclusive way (e.g. cooperation, competition, social control, tradition, social change, power, authority interdependence, the division of labour, etc.).

Social learning was relatively straightforward in societies that were more hierarchical, homogenous and static. But societies have been unlike this in most European countries for several hundred years: they are complex, multi-faith, multi-lingual, increasingly diversified. And this process is accelerating rapidly as Europe changes in the post-1945 and the post-1989 situations. We have seen widespread social exclusiveness in many societies and lack of understanding/tolerance/inclusiveness towards outsiders or 'the other'. Social learning in these contexts requires not only acceptance of traditional norms, but understanding and security about their underlying values (rather than their superficial norms) and how they change and adapt, as well as an ability to view and understand the culture of other societies with whom we are increasingly likely to come into contact. Citizens – mature and young – need to develop and use skills of argumentation and discussion, social observation and reflection.

In this volume we show some of the different ways in which children and young people are now learning to understand the relationship between the individual and society. We have organised the book in what we see as four unfolding phases. In Part One – Chapters 2 (Spinthourakis and Katsillis) and Chapter 3 (Nowicka) – we begin with how children's social identity is formed by the family, school and learning process. The second part – Chapters 4 (Adalbjarnardóttir) and 5 (Krull and Kadajane) examines how children develop their social relationships in both formal and informal ways in the educational system. Part Three – Chapters 6 (Pramling Samuelsson and Emilson), 7 (Verkest) and 8 (Tutiaux-Guillon and Mejias) – analyses some of the specificities of social education at different ages. The final part – Chapters 9 (Dekker), 10 (Trigos-Santos) and 11 (Pergar Kuščer) examines the main issues of social exclusion in contemporary European society and how they influence children.

Our aim was to present these questions from the perspectives of different countries and disciplines. We invited pedagogues, sociologists and psychologists with experience of education and research to develop these issues, not to present research monographs but to offer chapters that provide a synoptic overview, summarising and surveying the field as a whole, but with references to varying practices across Europe. Our typical reader, we imagine, will be looking for an authoritative overview, with references to more detailed case studies, rather than a case study itself.

When discussing problems and issues of children's social learning and in analysing particular elements of social effects of the environment on their development, we must be aware of the strength of these effects. The environment moulds not only children's behaviours and habits. It also influences their attitudes, emotions, beliefs and their hierarchy of values, which in turn determine the development of identity. The pre-school period is here of primary importance, because the bases of social identity are formed at that time. As emphasised by theorists such as Erikson (1959, 1968) and Logan (1986), this is the stage in everybody's life when, following the category 'I' (fundamental to the development of personality), there appears the category 'we'. This expresses our ties with other people and enables identification with their objectives, values and principles of conduct.

The first part of this volume focuses on the formation and development of identity. Two chapters discuss the role of two most significant formal institutions influencing children's social identity – the family and school. In Chapter 2 Julia Spinthourakis and John Katsillis stress that the role of the family in the formation of children's social identity is critical. Behavioural, psychoanalytical and learning theories treat parents as teachers, who constitute models of attitudes and values. Their impact is realised through a series of mechanisms: firstly, by a process of categorisation, as they define the category of 'people who are like us', and thus help develop group identity; secondly, by identification they promote certain values and views; and thirdly, they use the process of comparison to develop respect for other people. When we realise that the vast majority of examples of stereotyping and discriminating behaviour are rooted in social and economic inequalities, then we see that the role of the family in 'leading a child towards society' is critical.

Schooling, as the second educational institution and that closest to the family, plays a significant role in establishing the relation between the individual and culture, Schools bear responsibility for preparing students for full participation in a plural society. The concept of 'oneself' and of 'friends' is essential for the processes of group self-definition, and the concept of the different – or of the alien – is basic to this process, because it is only the reference to 'others' that creates one's own image (Nikitorowicz). In Chapter 3 Marzena Nowicka develops a series of questions about the role of school in developing ties with others. These ties are of a dual character: on the one hand, they may manifest themselves in openness to other people and readiness to include them into our category 'we'. On the other hand, they may mean excluding the different, the alien, from our own reference group. The author refers to the educational experience of Poland, which was isolated for years behind the iron curtain and now is now gradually opening to 'the different'. These social changes are bringing about changes to the educational system, and to the role played by the school as an institution. Nowicka suggests that education towards 'the other' can help those in the younger generation in moulding their own identities and finding their own place in social reality. This is a problem of not only relationships between people but also systemic transformations and attempts – made by both teachers and students – at defining their place in the new situation.

Children's national identity develops through interaction. Their understanding of social codes and expectations, as well as the ability to respect them, has a considerable effect on the feeling of being accepted and the system of values on the one side, and establishing ties with the reference group on the other. Such relationships allow individuals to verify their opinions and social beliefs, and to lay down principles and rules that constitute the pivot of a social group. The process of moulding these values is especially interesting in open, democratic and pluralist societies where there are frequent clashes of views. It follows that it is important to understand these processes and their practical implications, because education may affect the development of inclusiveness-related attitudes. The chapters of Part Two emphasise the role of the student-teacher and student-student interactions in social learning and promoting openness towards others.

In Chapter 4 on teacher-student relationships Sigrún Adalbjarnardóttir stresses the interpersonal character of school education. Through this process, teachers are expected to prepare students for active participation in social life, while students are required to cope with various problems – school-related, social and emotional. These expectations of both teachers and students influence the relations that develop between them. These relationships may have a constructive or destructive effect on children's learning about the society and the positions occupied by relationships and self. Abalbjarnardottir discusses teaching styles and strategies that aim to promote such understanding and skills among students. She stresses how social relationships between teachers and students help students learn both 'by' and 'about' the self, about social relationships and about the values and rules of society. In creating a classroom atmosphere of mutual respect and care, the teacher serves as a model. Teachers who are challenging and caring, effective and responsible have much to teach us all about promoting students' citizenship awareness.

Edgar Krull and Tiiu Kadajane in Chapter 5 introduce and analyse issues of social relationships between students. They do so from two points of view: firstly, of developmental changes in students' social skills; and secondly, through teachers' opportunities for creating favourable conditions for these changes. The educational focus of this requires linking knowledge about developmental changes with knowledge of teachers' educational activities, which introduces a third theme – the uncovering of social structures in student groups. Developmental changes in social skills are approached as the development of friendship structures and of attitudes of mutual acceptance and respect between students. Various sociometrical approaches are analysed, providing teachers with methodologies and tools to uncover social relationships between students. The final theme of this chapter is supporting the development of students' social skills, discussing approaches to changing and modifying social relations between students.

Part Three presents the specific character of learning in the periods from kindergarten to secondary school. The three chapters are by authors who represent a range of backgrounds, combining academic knowledge with practical experience: pre-school and school teachers and teachers of philosophy and history. Education is thus viewed not only from the perspective of developmental change, but also that of different experience.

Children starting in the educational system have to build systems of knowledge about the social world. They do this on the basis of experiences acquired at home and at school, as well as their own more private experiences and activities. The interaction between child and group results in learning and growth. How the child is included or excluded in the community of learners makes a difference for the child's future. In Chapter 6 Ingrid Pramling Samuelsson and Anette Emilson discuss children's social development and how contemporary research informs this, but they also raise the critical question of how to be an individual in the collectivity of the preschool and what preschool can do to foster children for the global society.

Looking at the specificity of learning at primary school we can observe the growing impact of holistic and personalising trends, in opposition to the more positivistic approaches that were popular in the past. In Chapter 7 Hugo Verkest presents an inspiring schoolwide strategy for social learning in the primary school, illustrated by many examples from daily classroom life and his own investigations. This strategy is based on two major assumptions. Firstly, it promotes caring about the child's proper functioning, not only in the classroom but also outside school. Positive role models are used to inspire altruism and support activity for the benefit of both school and local community. Secondly, it focuses on total moral development, aimed at values fostered by the teacher. Teacher's skills connected with the learning dialogue (as opposed to the teaching dialogue) are of special importance for a school wide strategy in social education. Verkest discusses also the areas and methods that are crucial in primary education, such as emotional factors, ecological factors, the factor of ethos, the *kairas* (decisive) factor and the visual factor.

In Chapter 8 Nicole Tutiaux-Guillon and Jane Mejias present a detailed analysis of learning about the society at secondary school. They confront students' understanding of social phenomena – such as work, family, social changes, social ties, rich and poor, and the course of society – with the way they are taught at school. The research shows that personal experiences play a fundamental role in understanding the social order. The knowledge gained at school is adjusted to accommodate personal understanding of the world, and is thus transformed in order to be completed. It follows that young people learn more and differently than they are taught, so that teachers should not only concentrate on the content of the message they convey but also 'imagine and implement new practices, link social experience and abstract frameworks, values and exact factual knowledge'.

Acquiring knowledge about society and trying to find our place in its structure are complex processes, burdened with particular problems. Some of these are personal, and others are social, concerning whole groups and societies. Part Four of this book deals with three issues of great importance to contemporary European societies and that are essential in social learning today: stereotypes and prejudice (Chapter 9), gender-related issues (Chapter 10) and the significance of social class (Chapter 11). Each of these is concerned with belonging to a group, that is, with the development of social identity, determined to a high degree by the family and school (as shown in the chapters by Spinthourakis and Kallis and Nowicka). Each of them also requires a transformation in social interactions, which in the case of education are student-student and student-teacher relations (as in the chapters by Adalbjarnardóttir and by Krull and Kadajane). And finally, each of them needs to be located in, and challenged in, educational provision at all levels, starting from preschool, through primary school to secondary school (as in the chapters by Pramling Samuelsson and Emilson, Verkest and Tutiaux-Guillon and Mejias).

Social experiences gathered at the first stage of our life are critical in the moulding of social attitudes. Negative attitudes are most often a consequence of negative experiences. They result from negative observations, stereotypes, clichés and negative feelings. In young people they follow from negative interactions and emotional transmissions acquired in the process of socialisation. In Chapter 9 Hank Dekker addresses the problem of racial and ethnic prejudice.

He presents the results of studies on prejudice against some European Union countries revealed by young Netherlanders, and contextualises this in a wider analysis of the literature. He discusses the psychological and sociological phenomena and mechanisms underlying ethnic prejudice, paying particular attention to inference theories such as cognitive models, including social categorisation, social comparison, and internal/external attribution processes, realistic group conflict theory, and affective models, including the emotional model and social identity theory.

Another widely discussed issue concerns gender and its influence on education, and the effects of education on gender-related issues, such as those of identity, social role and learning type. All gender analyses are based upon differences – active/passive, rational/ emotional, and so on. The issue is especially important in pluralist societies, where equal rights and equality of social opportunities for all citizens are of primary significance. But gender-related stereotypes are the strongest and most common forms of typecasting in all types of societies. Issues of gender and its role in social and civic education are addressed by Florbela Trigos-Santos in Chapter 10, in which she surveys trends with particular reference to educational experience in Portugal.

Experiences gained in early childhood are of great importance for the child's future, as are the educational conditions created by the family in the pre-school period. During the years of schooling the correlation between parents' aspirations and children's education is clearly visible. Due to both material factors (perhaps providing money for extra classes) and psychological factors (such as arousing intellectual curiosity, reading books, discussions), children from wealthier families appear to be in an advantaged situation. In most societies today, the perception of students with 'learning difficulties' is that they are disproportionately drawn from socially less advantaged environments. Their educational opportunities are lower when compared with other children. Many studies show that parental economic and financial status is a better predictor of a school success than is any measure of intelligence. The question of the effects of social class on social learning processes is examined by Marjanca Pergar Kuščer in Chapter 11. She focuses on the teacher's role in giving all students equality of opportunity, and her theoretical analysis of the influence of social class on educational attainment is illustrated by concrete examples from Slovenia.

This volume, part of the CiCe series *European Issues in Children's Identity and Citizenship*, produced in association with Trentham Books, brings together chapters and authors from multi- and mono-cultural societies, from EU member states and countries which are to join the Union in the near future. The experiences come from Western Europe and Central Europe and from its periphery, some-times even from countries geographically distant from continental Europe. This diversity makes the problems discussed more interest-ing. Our intention is to present not only a scientific debate but also a dialogue between people representing different cultures, whose experiences can serve the purpose of making the contemporary social order more understandable.

2

The role of family in the formation of social identity

Julia A. Spinthourakis and John M. Katsillis

Introduction

The composition and the role of the family have changed dramatically in recent times. The self-sufficient extended family of pre-industrial monocultural societies has little resemblance to the nuclear or permeable family of the post-industrial multicultural world, perhaps particularly so of Europe. Changes in the way families are organised and function have resulted in differentiated relationships that influence the development of children's social identity. It is difficult to ignore the changes to what is meant by 'family and caregivers' and to the notion of parenting in the 21st century. The role of parenting is no longer exclusively delegated to the traditional primary caregivers. Furthermore, geopolitical events have altered the cultural and ethnic composition of many societies, necessitating the development of new values and skills. All this has affected the manner in which the child is socialised, learns social skills and develops their social identity. The role of the family in the formation of children's social identity is critical. To examine this role, we will attempt in this chapter to outline social identity and then to examine the role of the family in the socialisation process as well as its influence on the formation of children's social identity.

Social Identity

Social identity refers to the way we perceive ourselves as members of groups. Since we may see ourselves as members of more than one group, our identity may vary depending on the group we identify with at any particular time. Each of these identities is accompanied by its commensurate beliefs, expectations and behaviours, defined by reference to the norms of the particular group. Identification with a group is only one of the three basic ideas of social identity theory (Tajfel and Turner, 1979), the other two being categorisation and comparison. Categorisation is needed to make sense of our social environment. We create categories using racial, ethnic, religious, occupational and other socially constructed categories that help organise our conception of our environment. The idea of social comparison is that in order to evaluate our group (and ourselves) we compare it with similar groups. Most of the time, group members tend to make comparisons in ways that reflect positively on themselves. They do this by using dimensions that are favourable to their group as the basis of comparison (McGarty et al., 1994).

All three ideas, and consequently the formation of social identity, are related to the society in which people exist. Furthermore individuals are, at least in part, socialised into their identities. Understanding that 'who we are' is socially constructed enables us to explain that how we and others see us is not fixed. Social circumstances, social learning and expectations create who we are and set our social identity.

Family, Socialisation and Social Identity

Socialisation is considered to be a process by which children and adults learn from others. It begins shortly after birth and continues throughout our lives. Socialisation occurs when infants and youngsters explore, play and discover the social world around them as well as when other people take actions designed to teach or train others (Baldwin, 2002).

It has been argued that childhood socialisation by the family has evolved over time from a focus on behavioural, psychoanalytic, and social learning theories, to viewing the parent in the role of the teacher (Wang *et al.*, 1999). Others suggest that parental involvement provides a framework that mediates the development and outcome of their child's socialisation (Darling and Steinberg, 1993; Hoover-Dempsey and Sandler, 1997; Maccoby, 1992; Okagaki and Frensch, 1998). The 'social capital' of the family (Coleman, 1988; 1990) arguably operates in a similar fashion. Social capital here refers to the quality and depth of relationships between people in a family or in a community and those relationships have the ability to foster the development of trust, reciprocity, norms, values, interactions and relations between children. Research has shown that everyday experiences in relationships with their parents are fundamental to children's developing social skills and by extension social learning (Cohn, Patterson, and Christopoulos, 1991; Parke and Ladd, 1992).

Whether as teachers, framework setters or interlocutors, family members exert great influence on the children. They are the most important determinants of children's behaviours, values and attitudes (Kagan, 1998). They are the individuals with whom the child first interacts, and from whom they learn the basic principles and conventions of life. Children spend nearly 70 per cent of their waking time outside school (Clark, 1990) and most of this is in the home, around family members. Learning begins at home and continues from there. Family members and especially parents are children's most significant others, and as such they influence children both as definers and as models (Katsillis, 1987; Scritchfield and Picou, 1982). Definers exert influence through the expectations they hold for the individual, whereas models influence by their behaviour and their accomplishments. In both cases, influence can be direct or indirect and, in some cases, unintentional.

The formation of social identity concerns that part of socialisation that refers to the categorisation, identification and comparison processes. Families have an important influence on the formation of their children's social identity in many and varied ways covering all three processes.

Many of the social categories that individuals come to accept and use are learned within the family. With increasing societal diversity, children learn at a very early age to recognise and expect a degree of variation and to accept that the world around them is made up of people who may be very different from them. By age three, many children can put their reactions to different skin pigmentations into words. They not only notice their own colouration but also mention how theirs is different from that of others. Just as they learn about colour and shape differences, children also begin to categorise people. Many three- and four-year-olds talk about physical differences between themselves and others. By the time children are in the early school grades, they have begun to consciously comprehend racial and ethnic differences. Most of these developments take place within the family and all are tied to the development of the child's identity (*California Tomorrow*, 2002). By defining these categories and those 'who are like us', the family helps develop the child's group identity based on religion, social values, shared language, ethnicity or national origin, or shared experiences of either a positive or negative nature.

Having a sense of group identity helps a child feel a sense of belonging. And the first and probably the strongest group identity is with the family. The identification with the family is self-evident: children tend to identify with their parents and to assume some of their qualities as their own (Kagan, 1998). The family's norms, values, and roles are also the first children learn and influence their behaviour for the rest of their lives.

Parents also guide their children – directly or by example – in respect to the comparison with 'others'. They influence the way in which children select the appropriate dimensions on which to compare their group and by doing so they help them develop a healthy sense of identity. The latter in turn helps children develop a sense of self-worth and be more optimistic, get along with their peers and do well in school. A healthy sense of identity also helps children be more open to people from other backgrounds because they are less likely to fear differences or put other children down to feel better about themselves.

Family and social identity in contemporary society

There seems to be little doubt that family has a profound effect on the formation of children's social identity. And it is this strong and multifaceted effect that makes the role of the family of paramount importance. The family's effect could be positive or negative. It may enhance the child's success and contribute to social cohesion or it might lead to marginalisation and social conflict (see Pergar Kuščer in Chapter 11).

Determining the elements and processes that result in the family having a positive effect on the formation of children's social identity is becoming increasingly more complex. Firstly, the form of the family today is more diverse than it has ever been and in a rapidly changing society new variants are very likely to emerge in the near future. The 'traditional' image of two biological parents with their children, living in harmony, does not present a very realistic framework for contemporary society. The contemporary family has many forms, ranging from the two-parent family, single parents, blended families, same-sex families, adoptive families – and the list goes on (Young, 2002). Bidwell and Vander Mey (2000) consider the term 'family' to refer to a collection of people, related to each other by marriage, ancestry, adoption, or affinity, who have a commitment to each other and a unique identity with each other, in which the adults in the group have varying degrees of responsibility for those young members that might be a part of the collection.

Along with the changes concerning the nature of what constitutes 'families and caregivers', another issue that has an impact on the development of social identity is race and culture. While what constitutes race may not be evolving, racial lines that were once considered inviolate are now in many societies crossed with far greater frequency than in the past. Individuals of mixed heritage – but not necessarily simply determined on the basis of 'race' – often identify themselves as multiracial. Some, whose parents are each of a different 'race', are 'biracial'; others comprise three 'races', because of multiple intermarriage by their ancestors over several generations, an increasingly common occurrence (Hall, 1996). Furthermore, because the designation has expanded over the years, individuals of a variety of types of mixed heritage that include ethnicity and culture (and with some who have extended the concept to include religion), now also consider themselves multiracial. Thus, following the pattern of multiracial examples presented by Schwartz (1998), we may see many different individuals of mixed backgrounds identifying themselves as multiracial: a child born in the Netherlands to a family comprised of an Indonesian mother and a Dutch father (two different ethnic identities; parents speak different languages; child speaks Dutch); a child born in the UK whose father is from Pakistan and whose mother is from Southern England (different ethnicities, races and languages); a child born in the Congo to a Greek father and a Congolese mother (different races, different ethnicities and different languages) and raised in Greece; a child born to an Algerian mother and a Ethiopian father and living Southern France. The combinations are endless, and all are viable.

Racial and ethnic group differences have a significant impact on children's social development (Anderson, 1999), although this impact varies with age and specific ethnicity. The children in the examples given above have a rich cultural heritage and a multiple and complex interplay of family influences, but some of them may publicly tend to choose a single ethnic identification, considering this politically correct, but privately cherish their multiracial heritage (Okun, 1996). The role of heritage in a child's development is affected by history, as well as by their social context and immediate environment. Herring (1992) points out that having a multiple ethnic heritage has a different and sometimes problematic effect on a child's development (also see Anderson, 1999). In addition, parents from different cultures may have different goals for the socialisation of their children, such as, for example, conflicting goals of competitive *versus* collective societies (Lynch and Hanson, 1992; Wang *et al.*, 1999). These differences may be evident in the different beliefs and parenting practices of different cultural groups.

Our knowledge concerning the socialisation of children in culturally diverse families or environments is still very limited. Despite a recent increase in the number of studies dealing with diverse cultures (Roopnarine and Carter, 1992), research in the field of family socialisation continues to be focused on investigation that involve white middle class Western samples (Darling and Steinberg, 1993; Wang *et al.*, 1999). As Stevenson (1991) observes, there has been little systematic exploration of the way prosocial behaviour develops in children from other cultures.

Things become even more complicated by the fact that individuals have multiple social identities. An individual may belong simultaneously to many different social groups and possess many social identities. Different social identities may become salient at different times, and in different situations, depending on the social context (Pittinsky *et al.*, 1999; also Roland-Levy and Ross, 2003). Each of these social identities is linked to a host of stereotypes about members of that particular identity group, and these identities – along with their related stereotypes – have a considerable influence on behaviour.

Usually, the more an individual's social identity is defined along stereotypical lines, the less likely they are to exhibit positive behaviour. However, some studies have shown that some stereotypes can even facilitate performance. For example, it was found that elderly people performed better when previously primed with positive stereotypes about the elderly (Pittinsky *et al.*, 1999; Levy, 1996). Another study found that Asian-American women performed better on a mathematics test when their ethnic identity was stressed, but worse when their gender identity was made salient (Shih *et al.*,

1999). This diversity makes the task of the family and, indeed, any other individual or institution entrusted with the socialisation of children, daunting. A widely supported view is that children succeed when they feel good about themselves and about their social identity. But how can the family or anyone else make children have a positive identity, when there is a multitude of such identities each of which may be used in a plethora of diverse social contexts?

Shih *et al.* (1999) suggest that this can be achieved by helping the children develop an adaptive identity. They found that a mal-adaptive identity is more susceptible to the negative influences of stereotypes and more likely to display negative affect toward that identity. In contrast, an adaptive identity allows individuals to choose between and within social categories those elements as well as to make those comparisons that maintain a positive affect toward their social identities. They claim that the positive effects of the adaptive identity are supported by most of the major identity theories and research. Self-categorisation theory and research has shown that people select those categories to which they belong that most contribute to a positive identity in a given context (Turner, 1987) and when membership in one category implies a negative social identity or is threatening, they may selectively increase the salience of other social categories to which they belong (Hogg and Abrams, 1988).

Self-affirmation theory and research have shown that when one dimension of the self is threatened, people are motivated to com-pensate by succeeding in another area (Steele, 1988). They suggest that at an intra-individual level enhancement might take the form of favouring an adaptive identity over a less adaptive or maladaptive one (Shih *et al.*, 1999). The same is true for the research on self-complexity. More specifically, this research suggests that the adaptiveness of an identity leads to a positive affect toward the identity (Linville, 1985; 1987). Individuals who have more com-plex self-representations may be protected from negative events because of the buffer offered by additional identities when one identity is adversely affected (Shih *et al.*, 1999).

Finally, self-enhancement research has shown that individuals make downward social comparisons to enhance self-esteem (Taylor and Lobel, 1989; Wills, 1981; 1983) and they sometimes even fabricate comparisons with others, if real comparisons are not available (Wood, 1989).

The role of parents in the development of children's identity

Parents can enhance the self-worth and the social identity of their children by helping them develop an adaptive identity. This may be done by either example or by guidance. However, developing such an adaptive identity may be a long-term process. The skills required are many and diverse, for they have to take account of a wide variety of social contexts and social identities, and these cannot be developed over a short period of time. Furthermore, simply teaching children how to act or react in different situations may be insufficient: a good deal of practice will be necessary. The children will need to come face to face with many diverse situations and to be guided, encouraged and supported before they can develop the ability to successfully adopt each identity.

Furthermore, if parents are to be successful in helping their children in acquiring the necessary skills and in developing appropriate strategies, the parents themselves must possess the appropriate strategies and skills. This is not always the case. And it may be that those parents who need these strategies and skills most are the least likely to possess them, because the most likely targets of stereotypes are usually socially and economically disadvantaged groups and ethnic, cultural and racial minorities. One way out of this impasse may be for other agencies or individuals, such as schools and teachers, to assume this task and work more deliberately toward the development of adaptive identities for their students and especially those who need them most. A more effective way may be to combine this with a programme that helps families develop adaptive identities. But this requires hard effort and considerable resources – and these are rarely afforded to the disadvantaged segments of society.

3

The role of school in acquiring social identity by children: searching for a new image of Polish education

Marzenna Nowicka

Introduction

1989 is one of the most significant dates in Poland's history, the year in which communist rule was overthrown in our country. It initiated a radical transformation in the country's development. From the ruins of the socialist utopia we began to create a new political and economic order, of capitalism supported by a pluralist democracy, a transformation which created a gap between new social needs and the means to satisfy them. These changes necessarily affected education. The break with socialism included ending central and bureaucratic education management and the party's domination of the direction and aims of education. Socialisation had been ideological indoctrination. School prepared pupils for their principal roles – as citizens, workers, consumers, ideological and political participants, co-producers of culture, team members and social partners (Muszyński, 1976). Polish school inculcated the basic norms of respect, patriotism, honesty and diligence (Janowski, 1988) through authoritarian educational methods to 'mould' or 'form' the student to a uniform template, through compulsion and symbolic abuse. The school curricula reflected state-promoted national homogeneity, levelling differences between people to standardise society. Many issues were avoided in school: for example, the political and economic liberties of ethnic minorities, the rights of the disabled to participation in education and social life, and the rights of other cultures. Educational institutions were institutions to reproduce and strengthen stereotypes, and created dislike, lack of understanding and the rejection of difference.

The transformations of the 1990s led to many changes in direction in education, some official, others local. From the government, the 1999 reforms of the education system included updating the curricula, introducing religious education, facilitating non-state schools, guaranteeing greater independence for schools and teachers (in curriculum and in teaching methods), and the local government of schools. Local and spontaneous changes included designing independent curricula, classes and schools. Both kinds of transformations were responses to contemporary social challenges and reflected a search for a new image of school, focusing on preparation for life in a dynamically changing and diversified society.

As early as ten, Polish children have firm, strongly negative and persistent attitudes to most minority groups in the country – Gypsies, Jews, Russians, Romanians, and those from Eastern Europe and the Balkans (Weigl, 1999, p. 57). This is surprising, because Poland is nearly totally homogenous: 'The number of national minorities is estimated at mere 3% of the total population of the country' (Łodziński, 1995, p. 121). This stereotyping is linked to lack of information about others, and children of between seven and twelve have very poor knowledge about national and religious minorities. The best-known nationalities are Germans, English, French and Americans, rather than our geographical neighbours. Minorities such as the Ukrainians or Jews are mentioned no more often than the culturally and geographically remote Japanese or Vietnamese. Apart from Catholicism, the children do not know of other religions, often confusing them with the beliefs of the ancient Greeks and Romans (Krzywosz-Rynkiewicz et al., 2001, pp. 60–66). These views are just as prevalent in the borderland areas, where the presence of other cultures is more obvious:

children of eight and nine living near the Polish border with Byelorussia have many gaps and errors in their knowledge of the religion and origins of their neighbours, and the vast majority select someone of the same religion as their best friend (Misiejuk, 1995).

The processes of democratisation are changing Poland into a multicultural society, and education has the role of preparing future generations to live and cooperate in this. There is now a clear presence of various languages, ethnic, national, religious and other groups in our country. The processes of globalisation and cultural pluralism have followed Poland opening up to the world. This leads to two key aspects of Polish education: cherishing the national tradition and strengthening student's social identity and developing positive attitudes towards those who are 'different' and engaging in dialogue with 'the other'.

This chapter considers the school's contribution in preparing children to function in a multicultural society, using Polish schools as an example. Education towards 'the other' is provided both through special independent curricula and through mass general state education set out in the recent reforms. The independent programmes have short-term and long-term dimensions, considered in the first section. Mass state education is examined through the approaches of textbooks to difference, through teacher's class activities, and through school strategies. The chapter concludes with a reflection on perspectives for education towards 'the other': Poland offers a particularly significant example, because of both the rate and nature of change and its particular homogeneous composition.

Special independent educational programmes towards 'the other'

While there are no specific programmes in Poland to prepare students for the conditions of cultural difference, education responds to the social transformation that is occurring. Individual initiatives are creating various educational programmes towards 'the other', mainly in non-state schools, but also in some state schools. Two types of programmes can be distinguished: short initiatives, repeated in different institutions and longer form or even permanent ventures in a particular school. Examples of both types of socialisation in Polish schools follow.

Education towards the other – short-term programmes

To illustrate the core of short-term independent programmes to prepare children to interact with 'the other', the first example comes from work on the Polish-Byelorussian border. Misiejuk (1999) has developed a programme for children living in a multi-cultural environment entitled 'Me and the Different'. This has been carried out in a couple of schools and kindergartens in the Białystok region. Misiejuk distinguishes different elements of activity. The first concerns awareness and recognition of one's own cultural identity, and the mutual acceptance of the qualities and attitudes of the group. The second element focuses on children's understanding of cultural similarities and differences: they learn to interpret the codes of various cultures at the level of language, religious rituals and everyday life behaviour. The third element includes analysing communication processes and inter-group relations, allowing effective individual action in a diverse cultural environment. This concerns understanding issues of injustice, denial of rights and unequal chances. The fourth element formulates new and creative solutions to personal and social relations: pupils had to establish amicable and harmonious co-existence. This was closely linked to the final element, which developed positive attitudes to the self and to other ethno-cultural and racial groups. These general guidelines gave kindergarten teachers three groups of issues for children. The first focused on the physical and emotional *I,* and the second dealt with the family and kindergarten group, that is *We.* The third programme had a segment called 'The Different', which raised issues of different cultures and customs. In school, teachers extended the scope to topics such as 'Everybody Can Be Different', 'What is it like to be Different?', 'Getting to Know Each Other' or 'Learning to Negotiate'. These were either organised so that the teachers presented 'the other' to children through static media, such as books, films or albums, while the other group introduced dissimilarity in an active way, primarily appealing to emotions rather than the intellect. Misiejuk found the latter more efficient: moving from 'the issue of "the other" as a distant and exotic being, to "the other" as a close and friendly one living among us' (Misiejuk, 1999, p. 111). Actively presenting dissimilarity helped the pupils recognise genuine social reality, injustice and lack of equal opportunities. The children's interest in and discussion of cultural dissimilarity, approached as a complex phenomenon, was evident.

A second approach to diversity in the social world, of a more psychological orientation, was suggested by Weigl and Łukaszewski. They developed activity scenarios to modify children's stereotypes and bias, used in schools with children between seven and ten in Opole and Białystok (Weigl and Łukaszewski, 1992; Czykwin; 1999). Five programmes were developed, each of five lesson-length sessions. Each aimed to make children aware of fundamental similarities between people, regardless of their social category, and of the diversity within each category. The 'Dreaming' programme modified attitudes to others through drama and imagination, through short sketches such as *A New Student, A Stranger Loses His Wallet, Guiding the Blind Across the Street,* and *A Summer Camp with Handicapped Children.* The programme 'I – We' (Social Identity) let students experience of 'I' as a simultaneously component of many 'We' communities, through scenarios such as *We Who Like Playing, We Who Like Sweets,* and *Who Are We?* The third programme, 'Universal similarity', demonstrated the similarities which link all children in the world, perceiving, describing and experiencing the world at sensual, physical and social levels. The programme 'Similarity between Emotional Experiences' enabled children to accept others – especially those seen as different in a racial, ethnic, physical or religious sense. They experienced feelings of unity, solidarity and the similarity of emotions experienced by everyone. The fifth programme showed the children the diversity that existing within each category of people (Weigl, 1999, pp. 91–111).

These examples of one-off programmes can significantly prepare students for good interactions with 'the other'. Their particular advantage is that they can be used with various age groups and repeated at different types of institutions. However, teachers in mass state education rarely use these sorts of activities.

Education towards the other – long-term initiatives
There are also examples of long-term initiatives, planned as more permanent contributions, primarily found in the non-public sector of education, which have greater flexibility in both curriculum and teaching methods. An example of such an institution which focuses on cross-cultural issues is the Tak Primary School of the Society of Alternative Education in Opole, with its multicultural educational programme 'Let's meet the Other – Don't let them be Strangers', developed by Maliszkiewicz and Weigl (1998). This has the intention of enabling children to approach cultural minorities in Poland and to examine forms of dissimilarity, such as religion. Each class, at each stage of education, is introduced to information about national minorities and their culture, taking some three months to introduce each minority – Byelorussian, Bohemian, Lithuanian, German and Jewish. Thus the Polish language and literature curriculum introduces fairy tales, short stories and the poetry of each minority; the history curriculum includes elements of each nation's history and how some of its members were living in Poland; there was often a link in geography through map work; and in Religious Education faith, religion, and celebrations of each group are discussed. The various 'national' characteristics are sometimes included in science classes, mathematics, physics and chemistry. Artistic activities, such as arts, music, theatre and dance, create opportunities for games, creative activity and self-expression of the students. Each cycle devoted to a minority ended with an informal 'national evening' party, organised outside the school, at which there were minority representatives, students' families and school

friends. The evening featured a national dish, prepared by the children, and outdoor activities and games (Weigl and Maliszkiewicz, 1998, pp. 76–77).

The focus in the Tak school programme was to reduce feelings of strangeness towards others, diminishing psychological distance and reducing negative emotions. An important component was to arrange situations in which students could experience similarities to others at the interpersonal level: what makes us similar is common ways of behaving, of emotional feeling, and of imagining the world. Opportunities were created for symbolic contact – through fantasy and role-play – with members of groups hitherto seen in a negative way. Pupils were able to discover the diversity of those within a particular category, as the view that all members of 'the other' are the same is a basic source of stereotyping and prejudice. The positive effects of cooperation – and the disadvantages of competition – countered hostility and dislike (p. 196).

Another institution with a similar programme is the school in Sejny, a small town at the north-east frontier of Poland. A fund established by educators, psychologists and teachers, called 'Border of Arts and Cultures of the Nation', supports the school: the fund focuses on the multinational and multi-religious integration of the Polish, Lithuanian and Byelorussian communities in the regions. Tolerance is taught through knowledge of one's own and one's neighbours culture, tradition and customs.

An example of education for cultural difference from central Poland is seen in the work of the Raoul Wallenberg School in Warsaw. Their 'The Neighbours' programme enables students to actively encounter the cultures of different nationalities, and of the handicapped, through personal contacts and experiences.

The final example of a non-state school preparing their students to live in a culturally diversified society demonstrates learning about 'the other' on the margins of the core curriculum. The Żak Independent Primary School in Olsztyn, established by Klus-Stańska, aims to extend students' knowledge of national, religious, physical, mental and economic differences. Interpersonal competencies are developed in the first grades through direct contact, such as meetings in school with non-Poles and members of ethnic minority groups, celebrating Children' Day with deaf children, and cooperation with the local children's home. However, the most important factor in socialising for a culturally diversified world is the school emphasis on students individually constructing meaning through negotiation, confrontation and definition in each new context. This breaks from the idea that the function of school is to transfer ready-made 'correct' knowledge, through passive perpetuation and reproduction (Klus-Stańska, 2000, pp. 10–11). The school has focused on a multi-directional approach to reality so students acquire the competence to function in the diversified world. Issues are analysed at many levels from the earliest age. Thus, in studying the family they move beyond the typical Polish family to consider one-parent families and families in Third World countries. As will be seen, this is not the norm in Polish schools.

One strategy to understanding the social world included asking questions at the beginning of the school day: in a study of the homeless, questions might be asked 'Who are the homeless?', 'Why don't they have their own homes?', 'How did you know people are homeless?' and 'How are they treated by other people?'. No subjects are presented from a monocultural perspective: even discussing a topic such as the autumn might include consideration of how the seasons are differently in other parts of the world. Another strategy to experience the complexity of the social world was 'intercrossing', or reversing the perspectives of meaning. For example, in an analysis of the novel *Tom Sawyer*, students formed separate groups to develop convincing arguments in the roles of Tom and Aunt Polly. This break with clear-cut interpretations helped make students aware of filters of perception when viewing social reality, particularly filters of cultural egocentrism. Thus an analysis in class of H. Sienkiewicz's *In the Desert and in the Jungle* was used to express theories of how different social groups are perceived, and possible perspectives to interpret the novel.

Students were asked their own opinions, as Europeans, on the African warriors in photographs in the novel. Social reality became genuine and complex, and a preparation for effective communication with different cultures.

These examples of educational programmes about 'the other' reveal an important point. Education can directly confront students with different types of dissimilarity (for example, the school in Opole) or alternate student and teacher activities (the Żak proposal). In the first case the focus is on learning about a wide range of dissimilarity, while the second has a more universal dimension, and sees dissimilarity as not necessarily strangeness. It may depend on the social context or environment of the school: the first type may be useful in the border areas or in religious or nationally diverse communities, and the second more in more general contemporary society.

Education about 'the other' in state schools

The examples analysed so far are in the non-public sector of education: we now turn to education about 'the other' in state school activities. The pluralisation of the Polish society is reflected in curriculum changes to include cross-cultural education. The requirements for I to III grades are specified very generally: the Educational Aims state that children should acquire 'an ability to make and maintain appropriate contacts with other children, adults, disabled persons, representatives of other races and religions, etc.' (Biblioteczka Reformy, 1999, p. 16). Other parts introduce the child to basic communities such as the family, the local environment and the homeland, together with the history of these communities, their typical customs, traditions and symbols. The content of the curriculum includes 'the life of children in other countries', 'similarities and differences between people; understanding versus tolerance' and 'diversity of heritage and exploration of culture' (pp. 17–19). The Ministry has approved over 40 programmes at primary school level, accompanied by textbooks: one can currently find many different textbooks.

How are these recommendations achieved in state schools? In a pilot survey I have analysed the contents of the most popular textbooks from five publishers, for each of the I to III grades. This is followed by a collection and analysis of teaching plans about 'the other' written by 69 primary school teachers – all with as least five years' teaching experience.

The content of textbooks and 'the other'

Textbooks are an important tool for the transmission of attitudes towards cultural dissimilarities. Usually treated by the teacher as the only source of some information, they are an important means to mould mental images: 'the literary material from the children's magazines and school reading materials can activate, shape and intensify a negative attitude towards "the other"' (Weigl, 1999, p. 141).

Texts for children from seven to nine years of age that develop openness, tolerance and acceptance of cultural difference toward 'the other' are at last appearing in Poland. They can be divided into texts on ethnic and national difference and texts on issues of religion, disability and other kinds of difference. But the mere presence of such texts is not enough, particularly as an analysis of their content demonstrates some shortcomings.

What kind of social reality about 'the other' do the authors of these texts present? The extent of diversity will depend on the book chosen by the teacher for a particular class. State schools rarely handle these issues, and the teacher's selection of the curriculum and text will determine the issues discussed in class. Textbook authors are selective about questions of social difference, and while one book may emphasise selected ethnic minorities and present their culture from a wide perspective, another may focus on disabled children. While the trend to presenting humanity as heterogeneous should be regarded positively, if the issue of 'the other' is not explored comprehensively it will not enable children to note dissimilarity at this level.

In books on different nationalities, content predominates: information texts, poems, national symbols and holidays, legends and myths, the country's origin and the establishment of cities. This is also so about Poland itself: texts stress significant historical events and sights of the main Polish cities. These issues are emphasised in books for each grade of primary school, and Poland is thus presented as an homogenous monolith, with information about the child's hometown in the background and less important. Conversations with third-grade pupils at an Olsztyn primary school suggests that they know more about the legend on the foundation of Warsaw than they know about their own town. They can list numerous sights in the capital, but wouldn't know what to show a tourist in their hometown.

The authors attempt to present Poland and the Poles in an international context. With basic information on the European Union there are customs of various nations and external differences and similarities. But most of this learning about the life and customs is primarily about those nations about whom we are not biased – the French, Swedish, Germans, Americans or Australians. Missing from these studies are Poland's nearest neighbours – the Lithuanians, Byelorussians, Ukrainians and Slovaks. It is hard to shape positive relations with these immediate neighbours without relevant core information. National minorities are handled cursorily. Sometimes unintentional stereotypes are reinforced. For example, in one books a nasty incident in a class is described: children run after a schoolmate calling him 'Jew, Jew!' Shocked, the teacher stops them, and asks the victim if he is upset by this behaviour. The child answers that no one would be offended if a Polish child were called 'Pole, Pole!': the text suggests that Jews in our country should feel sorry for not being Polish. Other texts convey stereotypes about the life of Gypsies: one depicts a little girl who does nothing all day but dance. After a nasty injury she changes her behaviour, ashamed by the attitude of her family. The whole text associates Gypsies with indulging in dancing and being lazy. Teachers will need to be particularly sensitive to debunk these and similar stereotypes, and to discuss alternative points of view in class with children.

Texts for the youngest grades only present external differences between people: readers learn that one can have a different skin colour, be physically challenged, dress or live differently. This superficiality is enhanced by trivialisation: texts dealing with important issues are complemented with marginal questions that divert children from the core issues. For example, in a short story about the problems of a freckled red-haired girl, readers are asked to list the names she is called and to pay attention to their spelling.

Some books deal with questions of religion. But all the texts about religious festivals consider Catholic celebrations only; other religions and rites are ignored. The only differences mentioned refer to minor differences around customs at Easter and Christmas. Students are not presented with other religions, and are not told that some people have no religious beliefs. Such an approach leaves the student convinced of the homogeneity of the surrounding world and the universality of Catholicism.

Despite the latest reforms, Polish textbooks still characteristically present an idealised world. Social issues such as addiction, divorce, homelessness, unemployment, loneliness and social exclusion are not dealt with. There is a tendency to avoid real problems. Child-hood is depicted as a happy period during which all problems can be easily solved: there is no space for real emotions and feelings. The texts offer artificial models of behaviour, incompatible with reality. One text has a poem on Children's Day suggesting friend-ship with the children from Shanghai, Switzerland, France, and England: if it cannot be real, let it be at least imaginary. In another text the teacher takes a disabled child home from school in a wheel-chair, and cheerful children add 'We'll accompany her too. Let's go for a winter walk!' These books give students a view of school as the place which has nothing to do with their experiences – and where to pretend to have certain attitudes to satisfy the teacher. The unreality is confirmed by the illustrations: among children from all over the world there are Amerindians in feathers with a tipi in the background, Eskimos with igloos, and a Black boy, always next to the same type of hut. In the light of this, it is difficult to use Polish textbooks to shape real images of a socially diverse world. If a teacher focuses only on the content of these texts, they will prevent students from understanding the world from the perspective of 'the other'.

The teacher as a facilitator of education about 'the other'

How do Polish schools prepare students to live in a world of striking social diversity? Research suggests the professional group of teachers is characterised by a strong tendency to present the world to students as socially homogenous (Misiejuk, 1997, p. 112). This section reviews lesson plans for teaching about 'the other' written by teachers.

Cultural difference is still a new issue for Polish teachers. Handling issues of difference was problematic for them. The issues they suggest to introduce social diversity appear selected at random and to be dealt with cursorily. Most frequently they suggest dissimilarity as an element of a main subject taught over a few days. For example, one suggestion was 'Winter around us – summer in our hearts'. It was rare to take a single issue for a particular day: teachers showed great concern to include all subjects in the same topic each day, bringing in classes in Polish, Maths, Science and Arts. Having been forced for years to uncritically follow the State curriculum, they now try to stick to a new curriculum that integrates all subjects at the primary stage. This leads to handling social difference cursorily.

Analysis of the plans shows that teachers tend to search for universality and homogeneity of all children in their needs, desires and interests – they emphasise that children all over the world like playing tricks, are contrary and love games. But they also notice and stress dissimilarity in physical qualities such as the colour of skin or hair, clothing and height. Teachers' lesson plans include collective conclusions such as 'Although children from different parts of the world look different (they are of white, black or yellow race), they all act similarly: they like playing, making pranks or singing'. There is no attempt to discuss more profound differences: malnutrition, poverty, natural disasters, family relations or forced migrations. In very few cases the teacher suggests raising real and serious problems. The idyllic vision is predominant and teachers evidently think that the age of seven or eight is too young to talk about poverty or forced work. They do not want to admit that some of those problems are also experienced by Polish children.

Many suggestions concerned disability. Students were to approach the handicapped through drama and discussion of their everyday life. However, the pattern of encounter with the disabled was always the same: get to know – understand – help. Problems of the handicapped and the sick were introduced to stir the children's consciousness and offer help. Each lesson plan came to the question: how should one help the disabled? One teacher even came up with the slogan: 'A healthy man is a gift to the sick.' While children should be encouraged to help the disabled, the sick also constitute a gift to the healthy! The dominance of bringing help creates an illusory feeling of superiority, influence relations between the handicapped and the healthy. Teachers do not always realise that good intentions may have such consequences in children's thinking. Their own stereotypes and biases affect the formulation of questions in class, and thus children's perceptions of the world. Many plans pose questions such as 'Is it possible to make friends with a blind girl?' Such friendship poses a bigger problem for the teacher than for the child.

It is not just the subjects that teachers select but also the teaching style that is of significance. In the lesson plans analysed are examples which *prevent* students from preparing for contacts with 'the other'. The majority of plans suggest communicating through demanding, moralising and directive language. The teacher explains, highlights or summarises, as in the examples: 'the teacher has led the children to conclude that one should not laugh at other people' or be 'persuaded to accept the disabled'. Teachers also get stuck on making terms precise: if tolerance is discussed, students look up the term in a dictionary and note it down in their books. Extending student's vocabulary is important, but teachers do not use students' own experiences.

Inflexible communication is reinforced with content-related questions that call for the repetition of facts, or are arbitrary, general and vague: for example: 'What is friendship?', 'What do you think of the disabled?', and 'What do children of the world have in common?'

The lesson plans often include drawing up collective notes with the students, to summarise the main ideas discussed. Many teachers deliver ready-made records to be noted by children. Students are unlikely to tolerate dissimilarity of others if their teachers prefer unanimity and discourage different opinions. However, among the collected plans there were some that encouraged critical and creative thinking by students, asking for individual opinions and for confrontation with the views of the others, and these constituted a significant minority. Only a few suggested more dynamic forms of communication, such as discussions, brainstorming, decision making trees, creating mega-plans or posters.

School strategies of education about 'the other'

These examples of socialisation have included situations in which either the teacher did not identify 'the other' in her/his teaching, or acted as if social diversity did not require any particular educational action. Some of the collected lesson plans describe another school reality, where issues of dissimilarity became very important, such as when the student group included a child who was disabled, or a non-Catholic, or from another other nationality. In an attempt to integrate the group the teachers then applied various strategies: they might first aim at mutual acquaintanceship (such as organising the students to meet the parents of a handicapped child, or asking a non-Catholic child to tell the class about their religion). The teacher emphasises the qualities and skills of the child perceived as 'the other', aiming to reduce the distance of interpersonal contacts between 'the other' and the rest of the class. The children see that their classmate, though different, can read well, stick model planes, recite poems, and so on: 'I tried to show the children the boy's strengths in order to present him to hem as an interesting person. During kinaesthetic games I chose exercises that enabled him to show his fitness.'

A desirable behaviour towards 'the other' child was often rewarded: in most cases, teachers expressed oral approval; others were more elaborate – one encouraged students to help a child with cerebral palsy by awarding badges. Teachers used edifying talks to persuade children to adopt the 'right' attitude towards the child who was different: 'I had to conduct a series of talks to convince the children to accept the situation'. Some teachers established classroom customs around communication and celebrations: for example:

> We shook hands to greet each other and we sat down at a table to work together. Together, we made portraits of the classmates . . . we made presents for each other. There's a group custom of inviting celebrants into the circle of children: at first, the children sing the celebrant's favourite song, and then one by one, they wish him or her all the best and treat them with sweets. Jaś, the boy with cerebral palsy, was celebrating his name day . . . Some of the children wished him all the best kissing Jaś on the cheeks, the others were touching his hand, trying to shake it, while some of the others were avoiding physical contact.

These examples of strategies show teacher's individual explorations as to how best handle 'the other' in the classroom. From all the plans, one can conclude that teachers are not fully prepared to work on cross-cultural content in school. Educators, equipped with poorly developed textbooks, approach the issue with traditional methods, and in particular use the transmission of knowledge. But there is a contradiction in preparing a dialogue of cultures through a monologue. Being directive and persuasive in communicating with the class through talk and note taking (rather than using discussion) is clearly inconsistent with accepting pluralism. An occasional reference to dissimilarity, with random and cursory presentations, does not let teachers prepare students for constructive and creative contacts with different cultures.

Summary

The contemporary social reality of Polish society is that it is becoming more multicultural, and school, as the second institution of socialisation after the family, plays a significant role in establishing relations between the individual and different cultures. Schools have a responsibility to prepare students for participation in a plural society. Learning about those who are different can help young people in moulding their own identities and finding their place in the social world. Nikitorowicz emphasised 'the concept of self and friends is essential for the processes of group self-definition, and the concept of the other or the aliens is also basic to that process, as it is only by reference to others that one creates one's own image' (Nikitorowicz, 1999, p. 30).

But this chapter has shown that preparing children to live in conditions of cultural dissimilarity is still not recognised or developed in Poland. Those responsible for the latest education reforms have paid insufficient attention to this aspect, and this is particularly apparent in the brief comments in the Minimum Curriculum Requirements. Education about other cultures and norms in state schools relies on imperfect textbooks, which present the diversity of the world in a selective and cursory way, idealise interpersonal relationships and avoiding controversial social issues. These flaws are reflected in the teachers' work with students, as seen in the analysis of their lesson plans. These also show other shortcomings: the random approach to issues of social difference, the lack of a multi-aspect analysis, and over-directive communications. The situation in some non-public schools is different: socialisation activities focus on preparing students to live in a dynamic and changing society. Their successful independent programmes should set an example for the public sector of education.

The changing face of Polish education depends on many factors, some of which are identified in this chapter. It is first important to disseminate approaches to education for social diversity through the educational system, and to make it more significant in the curriculum. Support is needed for those rank and file programme initiatives which accentuate mutual acquaintanceship and under-standing of difference. A thorough and critical review of textbooks is needed to establish cross-cultural education on a sounder basis. But most important is to properly prepare teachers to provide education about 'the other', about social diversity, in schools. The institutions for teacher education and training should offer both theoretical and practical support. This is no easy task:

> the educator should be aware that he is not the manager of the only culture, supposed to only meet this culture's official requirements. He must be a critic of culture, ready to change and modify, as the aim of cross-cultural education is to develop the vision to prepare everyone, regardless of the culture or origin they represent, to live and co-exist in the world. We need to shape and preserve the culture of peace, throwing back the colonisation of the minds of the minority by the vast majority.
>
> (Nikitorowicz, 1997, pp. 105–106)

4

'Respect between teachers and students is the basis for all school work':[1] Teacher-student relationships

Sigrún Adalbjarnardóttir

Education at school is fundamentally interpersonal. Teachers are expected to promote students' general growth and to prepare them to participate actively in society (as seen in the various national curricula in each country). Accordingly, students are expected to deal with various challenging tasks: academic, social, ethical, and emotional. These expectations go hand in hand for both teachers and students, and require teacher-student relationships based on respect. Importantly, the nature of these relationships can be a significant motivator for work at school (Davis, 2001).

In this chapter, I focus on the key role that teachers play in organising constructive and meaningful experiences for their students, as they promote their students' social, ethical, and intellectual growth while learning about society, social relationships, and self. I discuss teaching styles and teaching strategies that aim to promote such understanding and skills among students. I stress that social relationships between teachers and students help students to learn both 'by' and 'about' self, social relationships, and the values and rules in the society. Accordingly, I discuss how both students and teachers perceive good teacher-student relationships.

The Challenge: 'In a democratic society we take it for granted that everyone gets the opportunity to participate'

The development of teacher-student relationships in the school context is a dynamic process, that is influenced by the values, beliefs, and skills of both student and teacher (e.g. Brophy and Good, 1974). From this perspective, both participate actively in developing the teacher-student relationship, bringing to it the relevant values and skills each holds. Fundamentally, however, the power relationships between teachers and students are unequal (Johnston and Lubomudrov, 1987). Reflecting these constraints, elementary-school students have been shown to propose more reciprocal strategies in solving interpersonal dilemmas with peers by more often taking each peer's perspective into account, but they propose more unilateral strategies when communicating with a teacher (Adalbjarnardóttir and Selman, 1989).

In teacher-student relationships, characterised by mutual expectations, students bring values from within their families; these can vary in the emphasis each places on values such as responsibility, punctuality, respect for others, and tolerance. Similarly, the teacher brings to the relationship various values and visions (e.g., Solomon *et al.*, 2000; Veugelers, 2000), which may differ in emphasis. For example, some teachers may feel the basis for their work with students is promoting their 'well-being' and ensuring 'that they respect each other at work and play', aiming to enhance students' 'positive self-image, good social competence, and mutual respect', as one elementary-school teacher put it. Others, however, may focus on 'teaching them some knowledge', seeing it as not their 'role to look after the students or to entertain them', as another elementary-school teacher said (Fridriksdóttir and Adalbjarnardóttir, 2002). To challenge these relationships, students enter them with different levels of social, ethical, emotional, and intellectual maturity. Similarly, teachers' levels of professional awareness may affect the quality of the teacher-student relationship, as well as their success in promoting students' growth (Adalbjarnardóttir, 1999).

In this light, it is important to trace the teachers' values and pedagogical ideas about teaching, and their attitudes towards students, as well as their view of their roles in promoting students' growth. And it is important to explore how the students perceive their teachers' styles and skills and how that understanding relates to their social and academic achievement. Below I chart some recent research in this area.

Students' Voices: 'The teacher is to students what the rain is to the field'[2]

Several recent studies have focused on how students perceive a good teacher (e.g. Khawajkiie, Muller, Niedermayer, and Jolis, 1996; Belton, 1996; Thomas and Montomery, 1998). For example, Khawajkiie and her colleagues (1996) asked over 500 students aged 8 to 12 in 50 countries 'What makes a good teacher?' They got many interesting and illustrative responses, among them the following. A child in Mexico said: 'The teacher is to students what the rain is to the field'. One in New Zealand said, 'A sense of love for hard work is fine, but without a sense of love for kids, it's all a waste of time'. One in Zimbabwe said, 'A teacher must not have any favourites and does not separate the poor from the rich and the not-so-intelligent from the intelligent'. 'They shouldn't be very strict and angry, because it makes children afraid of them and unwilling to go to school,' said a child from the Czech Republic. 'A good teacher gives not only the lessons, but much more than that; she gives us new ideas and explains to us our doubts. She makes the classes an amusement and not a prison,' said a child from Portugal. 'A good teacher is a guide who helps me cross the road of life; who always observes where I put my feet and if I make mistakes corrects me,' said a child from Italy. Finally, a child from Chile said, 'They should only teach good things with words and deeds because it is in childhood that one gets answers for the future'. These quotes illustrate the themes of '. . . who loves all of us', 'equality', '. . . not too strict', '. . . who helps us grow and develop', '. . . guides to the future', and '. . . is a role model to us'. Further, we notice from these thoughtful quotes how concerned the children are about the teacher being fair, caring, guiding, and a role model.

Similarly, in asking elementary-school children about what advice and rules they have for teachers, researchers (Thomas and Montgomery, 1998) found them to be concerned about the affective characteristics of teachers: they appreciate their being gentle, caring, understanding, and fun loving. The corresponding rules for teachers were: 'Don't yell,' 'Be kind,' 'Listen,' 'Be fair,' and 'Laugh sometimes' (p. 378). Another study (Teven and McCroskey, 1996) indicated that students who perceived their teachers as caring evaluated those teachers more positively, found the course content more interesting, and felt they had learned more in the course. Further, the middle-school students in a recent study by Askell-Williams and Lawson (2001) responded to the question, 'What are the features of interesting class lessons?' with answers that clustered around three issues: teachers, individual learning, and social learning. They said it was important that teachers be interested and nice, that they relax, control the class, and explain. They also commented on teachers' tempers, humour, and fairness.

Similarly, when adults are asked about the good teachers they remember from childhood, they emphasise teacher fairness, care, and respect, as well as how they motivated them to study (Ermenreksdóttir, 1951): 'The main reason I liked her so much was that she was always so just and fair towards us.' Another adult in the same study also mentioned respect and stressed that the nature of the teacher-student relationships can be a significant motivator for work at school: 'Because of her teaching method and manner I started to care about her and started to respect her. As a consequence, I got motivated to study. We, the students, obeyed her in every sense and that was more out of respect than fear.' A third respondent in this study also recalled how the teacher cultivated respect and motivation:

> What I think that my teacher did the best for me, is, he motivated me to learn; I saw the need to study and get educated. And he developed my respect for him. It was not restricted only to him, but was also directed towards the various human concerns that were discussed, towards life and me myself.

Teachers' voices: 'The most important thing is to respect each student as a human being'

As teachers respond to the various factors they consider important in their own teaching and what good teaching is about, one thread appears strikingly in many of their answers: establishing a positive relationship between the teacher and the students. This thread stands out as if it were bright red. It comes through whether you ask a teacher at kindergarten, elementary school or secondary school; and it comes through whether you ask teachers of languages, social sciences, or natural sciences (e.g., Ingvarsdóttir, 2003). However much the teachers differ in their ideas about what teaching should be about, and in their teaching styles and skills, the bottom line to them is creating good relationships with the students; otherwise learning will not take place.

We might have expected the red thread of 'good relationship' between teachers and students to come through less clearly among secondary teachers than among those in kindergartens and elementary schools. Their students are older, the teachers specialise in a subject matter, and they teach many classes. Thus, in general, they spend less time with the same students compared to teachers in kindergartens and elementary schools. In a recent study Ingvarsdóttir (2003) interviewed Icelandic foreign language teachers and natural science teachers of secondary students aged 16 to 20. She found that in spite of the differences in their theories about teaching and in their teaching styles and skills, every one of the fifteen teachers emphasised that without a good teacher-student relationship, there is little hope of learning. As one teacher phrased it, 'If you raise a wall between you and your students then you will get nothing across, no matter how much and hard you try.'

In reflecting on what makes a 'good relationship' between students and teachers, elementary teachers have valued mutual respect, trust, honesty, and sensitivity/delicacy (Adalbjarnardóttir, 1994). For example with regard to respect, a teacher called Katrín reported:

> It is important that the students learn to respect each other and simultaneously themselves. They have to learn to respect others in

order to be able to have successful social relationships. It is also important for their self-respect and self-image that they show each other respect . . . It is very important that the teacher be positive towards the students and interact with them respectfully. The most important thing is to respect each student as a human being: to discuss things with them on as equal a level as possible and to evaluate them on their own grounds in order for them to grow and feel they are of worth in life.

Katrín also emphasised that the teacher 'had to cultivate positive feelings towards the students, to be considerate, and to care about them.' She pointed out that this cultivation involved every single student:

This is not a problem regarding most children, but then there are those that may behave negatively and give very little. Then this cultivating period starts for the teacher, to cultivate herself towards the child and let herself care about him or her. (Fridriksdóttir and Adalbjarnardóttir, 2002)

As we notice, Kristín clearly emphasised not only mutual respect in the teacher-student relationships but also care (see Collinson, Killeavy, and Stephenson, 1999; Elbaz, 1992).

Other teachers have also emphasised the importance of respecting one another's different opinions and of showing tolerance. One said: 'We have different opinions, our background is different and we must respect that. We need to live together in this society and we need to show each other tolerance.' Another emphasised respect as related to promoting students' autonomy:

I view it as number one that the teacher respects each child and his or her opinions . . . because if we immediately start at school to beat their autonomy out of them, we cannot expect them to be independent individuals later in life. (Adalbjarnardóttir, 1994)

Other elementary teachers in the same study commonly mentioned 'mutual trust' as crucial for good teacher-student relationships. For example, a teacher called Elín reported:

I want them [the students] to feel able to trust me when something lies in their heart and they have a problem. They feel so much better

> if they can trust the grown-ups they have. They need that and they show they want to trust us. Having that security they feel better and are more able to concentrate and work . . . and I have to feel I can trust them, to treat each other fairly and to contribute in their work . . .

Other teachers related trust to being honest. For example, María said:

> I want them to be honest with me. I try to be honest with them and I want them to be honest: that I can trust that they are telling the truth, that they do not lie to me to try to hide behind something even though it is something negative they have to report. In other words, I actually demand that they be honest.

Related to these statements, the teachers emphasised how essential it is that students and teacher be sensitive to each other's thoughts and feelings. 'The better the relationship we acquire, the better and more enjoyable the schoolwork will be', one said.

That these Icelandic teachers emphasise respect as a base for good teacher-student relationships corroborates findings in other studies, like the one Collinson and her colleagues (1999) conducted in the United Kingdom, the Republic of Ireland, and the United States. In this study, exemplary teachers saw respect as a vital foundation of classroom relationships and a base for effective teaching. They also interpreted respect as an important aspect of 'an ethic of care' (p. 350). The caring teachers respected each student as an independent individual, not only by 'being welcoming and sincere' but also by seeing the 'need to challenge them, to give them the sense that they are individuals with needs, skills' (p. 362), as one UK teacher phrased it. In order to promote the students' growth, caring teachers tried not only to increase their students' academic competence but also to know them as people and to develop their relationships with them.

In the expressions above from both students and teachers about good teacher-student relationships we notice the same red threads of respect, care, and fairness. Supporting this observation, DeVries

(2001, p. 153), who advocates for constructivist approaches in teaching, claims that 'the most essential aspect of the constructivist socio-moral atmosphere is a cooperative teacher-child relationship characterised by mutual affection and mutual respect.' Not surprisingly, teachers' actual perceptions of their interactions with students affect the students' perceptions, which in turn affect teachers' perceptions (Newby, Rickards, and Fisher, 2001).

Teaching styles: 'I feel my role is to guide the students instead of being dominating'

While she was attending an intervention programme that focused on fostering students' socio-moral and interpersonal growth, a teacher called Dísa expressed her concern about her authoritarian style when she got upset about student behaviour; she said she too often blamed the children, scolded them, and even shouted at them (Adalbjarnardóttir, 1994). We found Dísa was willing to reflect on the interpersonal aspects of her teaching, both with respect to her interpersonal style and her teaching skills (Adalbjarnardóttir and Selman, 1997). In fact, we found she was rather hard on herself in these descriptions, as we observed her to be an affectionate teacher who was warm and friendly towards the students, although she was also quite firm and occasionally showed her disapproval in unilateral ways. During the programme she noticed that she moved from using an authoritarian style (for example, scolding students) toward an authoritative style (such as requesting discussion among the students) as reflected in her comments:

> Instead of scolding the boys for their misbehaviour I started to try to get them to view the issues from various perspectives: What do other children think about this issue, what do they themselves think and what does the teacher think?

Dísa was responding to the findings of a study she participated in as part of the intervention programme; it indicated that teachers who received training like she did in working constructively with their students on socio-moral and interpersonal issues in the classroom were able to improve their students' social competence more than teachers who did not participate in the programme (Adalbjarnardóttir, 1993). More precisely, students in the intervention programme showed greater progress in reciprocity: they more often considered both participants' perspectives when trying to resolve hypothetical classroom conflicts compared to students in the regular programme. For example, they would suggest arguing instead of fighting, asking questions instead of commanding, and engaging in a discussion instead of a quarrel. Also, in real-life situations, the boys in the intervention group seemed to progress more than the boys in the regular programme. As we observe from Dísa's reflection on her improved interactions with the boys, these findings did not surprise her.

Several studies indicate that student relationships with teachers are associated with their academic and social achievement, such as their social competence and pro-social behaviour in the classroom. This has been found both in early childhood (e.g., Birch and Ladd, 1996; Pianta and Steinberg, 1992), and through adolescence (e.g., Ryan, Stiller, and Lynch, 1994). For example, Birch and Ladd found that young children's adjustment to school was associated with teacher-student relationships characterised by warmth, the absence of conflict, and open communication. On the other hand, Blankemeyer and her colleagues (Blankemeyer, Flannery, and Vazsonyi, 2002) found that among students aged 8 to 10, especially boys, negative perceptions of their relationships with teachers were related to poor school adjustment with regard to social competence.

In another study (Lewis, 2001), students in both elementary and secondary schools felt that teachers who reacted to classroom misbehaviour by increasing their use of coercive discipline inhibited their development of responsibility and distracted them from their school work. On the other hand, young adolescents who found their teachers supportive and felt more connected to the school tended to feel more competent and more task-focused as they pursued academic goals; they also showed higher academic achievement (Roeser, Midgley, and Urdan, 1996). Similarly, young adolescents who perceived their teachers as caring and supportive were more likely to pursue both social and academic goals, such as being socially responsible, and to show mastery orientations towards learning, as well as expressing academic interest (Wentzel, 1997).

In combination, these findings indicate that the quality of teacher-student relationships, particularly students' perceptions of emotional and academic support from teachers, are related to their social and academic success.

In a recent interesting study of teaching styles and student adjustment in early adolescence, Wentzel (2002) asked students to rate teachers on four dimensions parallel to and based on Baumrind's (1971) pioneer work on parenting styles. These teacher dimensions were: rule setting (control); high expectations (maturity demands); negative feedback (lack of nurturing); and fairness (democratic communication). A fifth dimension was teacher motivation (teachers' modelling of motivation toward schoolwork). Students' adjustment was measured by their pursuit of social goals. That is, what did the students see themselves as trying to accomplish with regard to being *pro-social* (share, help) and *responsible* (follow classroom rules)? Did they show *interest* in class, and use *control beliefs* about why and how they could do well in school (mastery orientation)? Finally, how high was their *academic performance*? Importantly, among the teaching dimensions, high expectations for students related most strongly to students' adjustment. Students who felt their teachers had high expectations for them were more likely to score high on all five adjustment measures: they showed pursuit of pro-social goals and responsibility goals, more interest in class, and more mastery orientation, as well as earning higher classroom grades. Equally important, students who felt their teachers gave them negative feedback showed less pursuit of responsibility goals and earned lower grades. In addition, if they felt the teacher was rule setting they were more likely to show less interest in class. On the other hand, students who felt the teacher was fair and motivated showed more interest in class. Finally, those who experienced their teacher as being fair showed more mastery orientation.

These findings highlight the effectiveness of the 'guiding teaching style', or in Baumrind's terms the 'authoritative' style with high expectations for student maturity, being fair and using democratic communications in the classroom. Overall, Wentzel (2002, p. 298) argues, her findings indicate that 'students are motivated both socially and academically by expectations to perform to their full potential.'

Teaching Strategies: 'I saw that I had to help my students to acquire understanding of different perspectives in social relationships'

Whether we characterise teachers as guiding, authoritative, or caring, those who challenge their students – socially, ethically, and academically – show them respect (e.g., Collins *et al.*, 1999; Wentzel, 2002). Professionally aware teachers respect their students' individual voices; they respect their individual differences in levels of interest and competence; and they respect their individual differences in terms of gender and social and ethical background (Adalbjarnardóttir, 2001; Adalbjarnardóttir and Selman, 1997).

Good and Brophy (1997) argue that the way teachers work with their students depends on whether they adhere to a view of teaching as transmission (direct teaching, emphasising memorisation) or as social constructivism (discussions, encouraging different points of view, reflection and mutual understanding). Related to this classification, DeVries (2001) has found that students from constructivist classrooms show more maturity in interpersonal development and better school achievement compared with students from traditional or didactic classrooms.

Professionally competent teachers aim to respond to their students' individual voices and differences as they promote their emotional, social, and ethical growth, as well as academic growth. These growth factors are interwoven into students' citizenship awareness: their understanding of the function of society and how to be active members of it with both rights and duties. To respond to all these differences and dimensions, successful teachers use different tasks and teaching strategies that encourage various perspectives.

One major focus of professionally aware teachers is promoting students' perspective-taking ability, that is, the developing ability to differentiate and coordinate different perspectives (e.g., Adalbjarnardóttir and Selman, 1997; Oser, 1992; Power, Higgins, and Kohlberg, 1989). The perspective-taking ability, we argue, is the base for students' *understanding* of values and rules in societies, as well as for their *skills* in social relationships, such as in negotiating and coming to an agreement over conflicting interpersonal, social, and ethical issues (Adalbjarnardóttir and Selman, 1989; Selman, 1980).

Well aware that society is becoming more complex and multi-cultural, professionally competent teachers see an increased need to deal with various citizenship issues in the classroom. These teachers promote students' citizenship awareness by engaging them in many activities: social and moral discussions, conflict resolution, rule and decision making, as well as voting. They use teaching strategies that search for the students' opinions and experience, and encourage initiative and responsibility by welcoming students' ideas and encouraging them to reflect on different points of view. These teachers emphasise democratic discussions about various controversial issues to prepare students for life. They stress high-stakes issues and issues that interest students and are meaningful to them, such as freedom, prejudice, immigration, girls' and boys' social interactions, risk-taking behaviour, and environmental issues (e.g. Adalbjarnardóttir, 1993; DeVries, 2001; Flanagan and Faison, 2001; Oser, 1992; Power *et al.*, 1989).

These activities provide students with many opportunities. They receive a chance to raise various views, listen to each other, argue, debate, analyse the different perspectives, engage in conflict resolu-tion, and reach agreement. They have a chance to reach a sensible conclusion about what is right in various human situations, and to have an impact and see their suggestions work in practice. By having a say, students exercise their *rights* as citizens to have an opinion and to make a decision. Simultaneously, these teachers emphasise students' collaboration in making decisions and solving problems, fostering both their mutual *responsibility* and their ability to work toward shared goals with people different from themselves. Using these constructive and democratic teaching strategies, the teachers attempt to promote the students' citizenship awareness, their understanding of social and ethical values, and their understanding of their rights and duties.

Building a sense of school community: 'It's natural in our democratic society that children have the opportunity to take part'

In fostering students' citizenship awareness, several educators emphasise the importance for the students not only to feel they belong to the classroom community but also to have a sense of the school as a community. A study conducted in seven countries, including Sweden, Hungary, Bulgaria, the Czech Republic, and Russia, suggests that a sense of membership and solidarity among peers that cuts across cliques in a school can play a role in getting adolescents to identify 'with a common good' (Flanagan *et al.*, 1998, p. 471).

One promising educational project that aims to develop a sense of community is the Child Development Project in the USA (Solomon *et al.*, 2000; Watson, Battistich, and Solomon, 1997). The project aims to create a sense of common purpose and a clear commitment to salient norms and values of caring, justice, responsibility, and learning. Its organisers emphasise a caring community of learners, with a school community characterised by caring and supportive interpersonal relationships, and collaboration among and between students, teachers, other staff, and parents. In this community, the aim is that students feel that teachers treat them fairly, that they feel close to people at school, and feel part of their school. With regard to teaching activities, the project emphasises opportunities for students to participate meaningfully in decision-making and other-wise be actively involved in the intellectual and social life of the classroom and school. In building up a sense of community, how-ever, they warn against de-emphasising academic learning: teachers should not neglect academics while community-building or try to show they are caring by accepting poor work from the students.

Their research has found the programme to have positive effects on students' sense of the school as a community and other school-related attitudes and motives (e.g. liking for school, achievement motivation); school attitudes, skills and values (e.g. concern for others, altruistic behaviour, conflict resolution skill, commitment to democratic values); and involvement in problem behaviours (i.e. reduced use of alcohol and marijuana, and less participation in some forms of delinquency, including violent behaviours such as 'gang fighting') (Solomon *et al.*, 2000). In short, in the project, 'sense of community' in school has been identified as a pivotal con-dition for children's ethical, social, and emotional development, and also for their academic motivation.

Discussion: 'See how human beings need much more understanding of each other's points of view?'

The research traced above emphasises the importance of respectful, trusting, and caring relationships between students and teachers as a base for successful work at school (e.g., Adalbjarnardóttir, 1993; Collins *et al.,* 1999; Wentzel, 2002). In creating a classroom atmosphere of mutual respect and care, the teacher serves as a model, or in the words of Stanulis and Manning (2002, p. 5), 'How much adults say, what they say, how they speak, to whom they talk, and how well they listen, all influence a child's estimation of self-worth and impressions students have about each other.'

Though we now know 'some things' about how both teaching styles and strategies relate to the students' social, ethical, and aca-demic achievement (e.g. DeVries, 2001; Wentzel, 2002), and how school community building helps promote this growth (e.g.

Solomon *et al.,* 2000), we need more research on how teachers' life stories, values, and pedagogical visions relate to their teaching styles and strategies in their daily work with their students as they learn about self, relationships, and society. Related to this, we need to study how teachers' life stories, values, and pedagogical visions affect the promotion of students' social, ethical, emotional, and academic growth, all of which are interwoven into their citizenship awareness. The outstanding concern is the professional competence of teachers. Teachers who are challenging and caring, effective and responsible have much to teach us all about promoting students' citizenship awareness. So do students who share their perceptions of good teachers.

Notes

1. The quotes in the chapter's title and subheadings are from a study of teachers' professional awareness (Adalbjarnardóttir, 1994).

2. This reflective and metaphorical quote is from Zaira Alexandra Rodriquez Guijarro, an 11 year-old Mexican girl (see Khawajkiie *et al.*, 1996).

5

The development of social relationship between students

Edgar Krull and Tiiu Kadajane

The development of social relations between students is an important aspect of their social growth and maturation. Wentzel and Caldwell (1997) showed that group membership is, over time, the most consistent predictor of student grades and that peer relationships are related indirectly to classroom achievement, through their relationship with prosocial behaviour. Ladd *et al.* (1996) demonstrated that it is the relational features of children's classroom friendships that yield broader psychological benefits or costs, and that in turn these affect children's development and social adjustment. The introduction of the dimensions of intrapersonal and interpersonal intelligences as indicators of social competence in Gardner's (1997) theory of multiple intelligences further indicates the importance of social self-awareness and readiness for interpersonal relations in the development of the most fundamental human characteristics.

In the normal development of child and student peer relations there is little need for adult intervention. But when, not that infrequently, children's relationships with their peers does not develop as expected, this can be the result either of personality factors related to the child or to particular factors in the child rearing practices in the family or in the school. Educators need a firm understanding of the major factors that influence the development of the capabilities for interpersonal relations, to be able to identify irregularities in this development, and to be able to use effective strategies for restoring the situation. This chapter briefly describes the development of peer relations, showing age-dependent changes in friendship structures, and then introduces some techniques that can be used to assess the quality of peer relationships. It concludes with a discussion of some intervention programmes that have been used to improving peer relations.

Development of social competence in children

Many psychologists have emphasised that perceptual and cognitive processes mediate social behaviour by influencing the child's inter-pretation of social cues (see, for example, Dodge *et al.*, 1986). An individual's interpretative power depends on both their emotional and their cognitive experiences and capabilities. As the cognitive experience of small children is largely yet to develop, their behaviour in their attachment to caregivers is thus largely deter-mined by emotional factors.

Neo-Darwinian theory suggests that emotions and cognition both serve the same end, namely of self-preservation. Thus Pluchik (1991) argues that in simple animals emotions are the cues to actions that have survival value, and in more complex animals, including human beings, cognitive capacities perform the same function, correcting or amplifying the predictions of the emotions. However, even with a high level of cognitive development, the experience of emotions in early social interactions with other people would play the most critical role in an individual's readiness for further social contacts. This view is supported by Erikson's (1968) theory of psychosocial crises, which claims that failure to solve initial emotional conflicts – such as that between *global trust* versus *mistrust*, at approximately the age of one year – will hamper the positive solution of all the individual's following emotional conflicts: *autonomy* versus *shame and doubt*; *initiative* versus *guilt*; and *industry* versus *inferiority*. This accumulated unconscious mis-trust of other people and a lack of self-confidence will interfere with the normal development of social skills in young people, and culminate in adolescence with the appearance of serious difficulties in the formation of identity.

As the most critical period in student social and emotional development is early childhood, it is clear that in cases of social underdevelopment and emotional maladjustment the student's earlier experience of social learning within the family should be considered.

Parenting influences

Research on the impact of parenting on children's social development usually describes two major scales of parental behaviour, represented by *love* versus *hostility* and *restrictiveness* versus *permissiveness* (Good and Brophy, 1995). While the love–hostility dimension is most closely related to child's self-esteem and orientation to others, the restrictiveness–permissiveness dimension is instead closely associated with the development of initiative, of autonomy, and of conformity. These two dimensions of parenting are not usually correlated with each other. Therefore four clear-cut parenting styles are possible, as combinations of extremist parenting behaviours on the two scales. Each of these parenting styles tends to produce quite different attitudinal dispositions and expectations towards other people's behaviour (Good and Brophy, 1995, pp. 92–93):

> *Love combined with permissiveness* – high self-esteem and sociability combined with independence and nonconformity. These children are often social leaders or are highly creative.
>
> *Restrictiveness combined with love* – conforming and good adjustment to parental demands. Usually these children are overly dependent on their parents, and lack creativeness and initiative.
>
> *Permissiveness combined with hostility* – hostility, aggressiveness and paranoia. The consequence of this parenting behaviour is usually low self-esteem in children, often disguised by openly aggressive behaviour.

Hostility combined with restrictiveness – low self-esteem, inhibitions, feelings of guilt and inadequacy, and general neurotic tendencies.

Educational practice suggests that high love with moderate permissiveness has the highest potential to produce a cheerful disposition, friendliness, emotional stability, sincerity and many other personality characteristics which are likely to make a student liked by his or her peers. These acquired personality traits have a strong impact on children's interpretations of their social world, enabling them to predict the behaviour of others, to control their own behaviour, and to regulate social interactions.

The development of these capabilities can be analysed in at least three interrelated aspects to give a deeper understanding of the development of friendship patterns in students (Erwin, 1993):

empathy and role-taking;

understanding of the concepts of friendship, and of the rules, obligations, and benefits of such a relationship; and

the attributions that children offer for the causes of social behaviour.

Development of empathetic capabilities

Hoffman's (1980, 1988) cognitive-affective theory of moral development describes the development of pro-social behaviour as occurring in four stages:

• Global empathy

• Egocentric empathy (1–3 years)

• Empathetic understanding of another's feelings (from early childhood to adolescence)

• Taking into consideration another's perspectives and the circumstances that caused the need for emphasizing.

These four stages of development represent a gradual perfection of the growth of empathetic understanding or of role taking – the ability to put oneself in the psychological place of another person. According Selman (1980), the young egocentric child, at stage zero of social role-taking, will see his or her friends simply as people who live nearby or are playmates. At stage one, the child recognises that his/her playmates have different emotions and intentions. Thus a friend becomes anyone who tries to do nice things to the child. By stage two, the child recognises that friendship implies a reciprocal relationship, with sharing, mutual respect, kindness and affection all contributing to this. The pre-adolescent, at stage three, has an awareness of the personalities and preferences of their peers, and a friend now becomes a person with similar interests and values, with whom there is mutual support and the sharing of intimate, personal information. Finally, the adolescents in stage four are entering a phase in which relationships show both interdependence and intimacy, while at the same time respecting the other's autonomy. Consequently, the generalised pattern of children's friendships is one in which they gradually become more selective and other-centred.

Understanding of friendship

Bigelow and La Gaipa (1975) and Bigelow (1977) asked school teachers to conduct class exercises in which American, Anglo-Canadian and Scottish children in grades one to eight (about 6–14 years of age) had to reflect on their best friends of the same sex and to write about what they expected of a best friend that was different from what they expected from other acquaintances. Content analysis of these pieces of writing revealed a sequential invariance of stages in the development of friendship expectations. Eleven categories of friendship expectations were identified, each appearing at a particular age levels and each increasing in intensity with age (Bigelow and La Gaipa, 1975):

Grade when category first observed	Categories of friendship expectations
2	Common activities (1) and helping (2) (friend as giver)
3	Stimulation value (physical attractiveness, neatness of dress, etc.) (3) and propinquity (living nearby) (4)
4	Character admiration (5), acceptance (6), and incremental prior interaction (7)
5	Loyalty (8) and commitment (9)
6	Genuineness (helping friends rather than being helped) (10)
7	Common interest and intimacy potential (11)

This study also suggested that the expectations of friendship in the more sophisticated stages do not imply that information that was significant at previous stages subsequently unimportant, but rather that it is superseded by new aspects of expectations. A more recent study by Niffenegger and Willer (1998) compared the behaviours that young children associate with friendship to what adults recall about the beginnings of enduring friendships. This supported earlier research that suggested that children's understanding of friendship evolves from concrete, behavioural relationships, based on sharing material goods and pleasurable activities.

Impact of attributions

Attributions are defined here as learned explanations which people give to the causes of their success or failure. Usually, when extremely pessimistic and subjective attributions are given to qualities of personality in the case of failure, this leads to further attitudes of self-blaming; while moderately positive attributions to personal qualities will lead to increasing self-confidence. A study of 660 fourth-grade students by Cillessen (1997) indicated that these children's perceptions of their peer relations played a mediating role in the link between peer status and later outcomes. In particular, negative social self-perceptions play a determining role in the relationship between low peer status and later anxiety – withdrawal, low academic achievement and loneliness. In general, studies of children's social relationships indicate that popular and unpopular children interpret other people's behaviour in different ways. Popular children are more accurate at recognising the social effects of their behaviour and regard their world as more subject to their own control (Erwin, 1993, p. 54). Conversely, rejected children overestimate their peers' evaluation of their social competence and tend to attribute social failure to their own personal inadequacy, rather than attributing rejection to situational factors or to other people. The attribution of social failure to personal incompetence is also associated with deterioration in using strategies to initiate relationships, particularly in comparison to those children who attribute rejection to the characteristics of the other child, or simply interpersonal factors such as incompatibility. For example, a study of fourth and fifth grade pupils by Goetz and Dweck (1980) showed that children with low peer status were more likely to give personal attributions of incompetence as an explanation for their rejection, thus pushing themselves into a cycle of self-blame and leading to feelings of helplessness.

General patterns of friendship during school years

Damon (1977) described the normal development of student friendship relations in three phases, in a model that integrates many research findings:

Phase one. Elementary school children (up to seven years) understand friendship relations in a self-centred and superficial manner. They are used to playing with peers of the same age and sex. Their friendship relations are overwhelmingly associated with sporting activities and entertainment: boys' activities are particularly related to sport, while girls' friendship relations tend to satisfy their needs for socialising. Friends are thus other children who customarily play with the child, who share their belongings and toys with him or her and who behave well with them. The main criteria advanced for deciding about friendship are the 'goodness' and the 'badness' of the other child. As young children's understanding of their own personal interests, values and attitudes and those of others are transient and lacking in depth, their friendship groups are often short-lived. Therefore, brief attachments of young children to one or another of their classmates is a common phenomenon in their social development.

Phase two. At this level of social development readiness to help a friend, or share goods with him or her becomes a major factor determining the friendship. Though the friends are still mostly play-mates, children begin to select friends on the basis of more specific and permanent personality traits. Typical justifications for making friends are 'She always gives me sweets when she buys them', 'He always protects me when other pupils tease me', and so on. The thinking that underlies this phase of understanding of friendship relations corresponds to the Piagetian stage of concrete operations, which enables pupils to foresee the possible consequences of their initiatives in making friendship relations.

Phase three. The quality of friendship relations reaches its highest level of development in adolescence. Young people take as a friend a person who shares common interests and values with them, with whom they can discuss intimate issues, and on whom they can rely when they are experiencing hardship. If the friendship relations at the former stage were based on common concrete activities, then at this stage of social development more abstract intellectual values underlie friendship. The creation of such friendship relations calls for an ability of operating abstract concepts and ideas. Young people's friendship relations become more permanent and they are not frightened by occasional incidents that earlier would lead to the collapse of friendship. In early adolescence friendships are usually made with young people of the same sex. At this age young people often consider relations with members of the peer group as more important than relations with their parents, because many of the interests and values of their peer group are closer than those of adults. After puberty, the importance of belonging to a peer group gradually declines and adolescents become more independent. Their interest in the opposite sex increases and they begin to pair off.

Assessment of students' social status and competence

Teachers can use both quantitative and qualitative methods to assess pupils' peer relations, their social status and their social competence. Relationships and group structures in peer groups are generally assessed using sociometric procedures.

The sociometric assessment of social status

In this procedure, members of a group evaluate each other against one or more criteria. For example, asking each student in a classroom to list the classmates he or she would most like to work with on a committee (or play with, study with, or invite to a birthday party, etc.) and then to list three other classmates with whom they would least want to involve in these activities.

Student choices are then tallied and each is assigned to a sociometric group. Usually the following criteria are used (Van Lieshout, 1998): children who have

- high acceptance and low rejection scores are classified as *popular*,

- high rejection and low acceptance scores as *rejected*,

- low social impact (low rejection and acceptance scores) are classified as *neglected*, and

- high social impact (high rejection and acceptance scores) as *controversial*.

Those who are average in all four dimensions form the fifth sociometric group of children – children with *average status*.

A meta-analysis of 41 studies carried out by Newcomb, Bukowski, and Patee (1993) showed more specific sociometric group differences, including aspects of aggression, sociability, withdrawal, and academic and intellectual abilities. A growing number of longitudinal studies are leading to the identification of developmental pathways, which may allow the relationship between early sociometric status and later personality development (Van Lieshout, 1998).

Another informative way to analyse the social relationships of a group of students is to compile a sociogram. This is a chart in which pupils are marked by symbols (for example small triangles stand for boys and circles for girls), with arrows between pairs of symbols used to graphically represent student nominations of their classmates. For classroom organisation purposes, it is usually sufficient to draw a single sociogram representing students' positive and negative nominations: this will uncover the social structure of the class and identify students at risk (Lindgren and Suter, 1985, p. 436–437). An appropriately designed sociogram will help the teacher to more objectively identify classroom leaders (those with several positive nominations), friendship circles and pairs (on the basis of mutual nominations) and neglected students (those who are not selected by others).

However, a sociogram remains only a tool to help discover neglected or rejected students: it will reveal nothing about the potential reasons for a student's low social status. Thus no con-clusions can be made about a student's lack of social maturity or of social adjustment based on a sociometric analysis, and further investigation will be required about a potentially at risk student. Conversely, a high measure of sociometric acceptability only shows a young person's level of popularity, and shows nothing about the quality of his or her social relationships (Hogan and Mankin, 1970).

Assessing social competence

An assessment of social competence in peer relations can be derived from several sources, including self and peer evaluation, parent's or teacher's judgments, observation of the child's inter-active behaviour, and an assessment of the child's social cognition. The correlations that are found between these various forms of assessments from different sources are typically moderate, staying between 0.30 and 0.40 (Van Lieshout, 1998). The reliability of single assessments from which to make objective conclusions about the social competence of a student is therefore rather low. More consistent information on a student's social and emotional adjustment, social skills and friendship relations can be gathered by keeping a diary of observational records when the indicative behaviours occur, and by generalising information from complementary sources.

Intervention for improving student social relations

The intervention of the teacher to improve a student' social skills and his or her competence in socialising with peers is usually needed when the conventional education of students and of the class as a social group does not ensure normal social development. Those students with social developmental difficulties are often those young people whose emotional and social development in the preschool period was disturbed; but also students who have experienced mistreatment by teachers or/and parents in the period at which they were of school age. Whatever the reason for such social immaturity, the underlying disturbances in emotional and social development are typically deeply ingrained by the time that parents or teachers discover that the child has difficulty in developing normal social relationships with their peers. By the beginning of puberty these students may have already developed rigid self-concepts of inadequacy about their social abilities, and may be trying to avoid situations that would reveal their (often self-invented) insufficiency. Such feelings of inadequacy set in motion a series of self-fulfilling prophecies, since those students who expect failure and rejection are likely to see in each difficult interaction with their peers the confirmation of their ill-founded expectations.

Backwardness in a student's development of social competence usually manifests itself as a negative determining tendency or bias in his or her behaviour, which penetrates all layers of his or her personality. This generalised mental set has been characterised by Krathwohl *et al.* as '. . . persistent and consistent response to family of related situations or objects.' They suggest 'it may often be an unconscious set which guides action without conscious forethought' (Krathwohl *et al.*, 1964, p. 184).

Social competence is a complex outcome of education, and if intervention is needed it presents a real challenge for teachers. Intervention calls for the creation of conditions that support the unlearning of negative personal attitudinal dispositions and learning of positive attitudes and new social skills necessary developing successful relationships with peers. To this end, all learning practices that develop components of social competence could be useful, because the progress and success achieved in one particular aspect of social capability may often be generalisable to other aspects. For this reason practically all intervention programmes – independently of the particular theory of learning on which they are based – give an at least temporary positive effect in helping socially immature students.

The structure of social competence

In understanding the strong and weak sides of different intervention programmes it is important to comprehend the structure of social competence, and in particular its main components and the underlying learning principles about independent and interactive development of the component elements. The analysis given above of the development of different aspects of social competence highlighted both the affective and cognitive aspects. A third aspect – the mastery of automatic social skills and of patterns of social performance – was not discussed above: although it can be seen as unimportant in contributing to general social development, it nevertheless plays a highly significant role in every incidence of social interaction. Consequently, the development of social competence requires students to develop all the main spheres human capabilities, as defined by Bloom and his colleagues within the affective, cognitive, and psychomotor domains of educational goals (Bloom, 1956).

As human behaviour is always influenced by – and in certain cases even started by – the attitudes and emotional condition of an individual, affective aspects deserve the close attention of teachers in promoting the social competence of students with social difficulties.

In the cognitive development of social competence it is important to discriminate between social skills and social competence. McFall defines *social skills* as representing the specific abilities required for competent performance. *Social competence*, on the other hand, is a general term about an evaluation of an individual's adequacy in certain social tasks (McFall, 1982). Whichever way social adequacy is defined, it is evident that competence is a function of both specific behavioural skills and situational, or task, demands.

The psychomotor aspect concerns the mastery of single performance skills as well as of automatic behavioural patterns. The development of all three aspects of social competence calls for different learning processes and for conditions of learning that will support them.

Behaviourist approaches

Educators have usually given the greatest attention to classical and instrumental behavioural learning theories and operative conditioning.

Classical conditioning, according to Pavlov (1927), is the repeated coincidence of a neutral stimulus with an unconditioned stimulus, causing basic emotions like fear and this duly leads to the condition where the initially neutral stimulus starts to cause similar reaction to the unconditioned stimulus. For example, a student who feels that she or he is being rejected and humiliated by peers when they attempt to socialise would develop a response of further avoidance of these contacts in similar situations. Intervention in such a case would be to remove this negative association between the cue, represented by interaction with the peer group, and the negative emotion. This can be achieved by providing the emotionally hampered student with positive experiences of interacting with peers. At the same time, training is needed in the social skills that were lacking, and whose absence caused the initial feelings of inferiority.

Training in specific social skills can take the lead in the law of effect (Thorndike, 1913), underlying instrumental conditioning.

Behaviour which is followed by a reward or by reinforcement is strengthened, while behaviour that is followed by negative consequences is weakened. The principle of shaping (Skinner, 1954), based on the theory of reinforcement of positive behaviour, gives many opportunities for gradually developing complex behavioural patterns. Many of the behavioural patterns needed to make contact with peers and to socialise with them could be developed by training under a teacher's guidance in less stressful conditions, to the point where they became automatic in their application. These skills might involve very different capabilities: starting with greeting the peer group and ending with the control of body stances and of language in the course of social interactions. Sometimes techniques of behaviour modification, based on reinforcing positive reaction and ignoring inappropriate reactions to a cue could be helpful. All approaches of a behaviourist intervention nature are aimed at the development or the modification of associative links between cues (stimuli) and reactions, thus providing the individual with the capacity to make automatic reactions to his or her physical and social environment.

Cognitive approaches

Cognitive theories of learning help explain the acquisition of the capabilities for information processing and understanding. These capabilities are often needed to correct initial emotional responses that would cause problematic reactions in interactions with other people. For example, understanding plays a major role in the development of a student's role-taking abilities, moving from egocentric empathy to taking another's perspective in to consideration. People's conscious social interactions are always based on their decision to behave in one way or another. For example, Wentzel and Erdley (1993) examined the relationship between having the knowledge of the strategies of making friends, prosocial and antisocial behaviour, and peer acceptance at school, in a sample of 423 sixth and seventh graders. They found that a knowledge of both appropriate and inappropriate strategies for making friends was related to both types of social behaviour and to peer acceptance.

Decisions to behave in one way or another in social interactions always have moral implications, and call for the actors to exercise moral judgement and value analysis. Therefore the methods used to promote student's moral judgements and their capabilities for analysing values can also be useful for developing students' social competencies.

Kohlberg (1984) considered the development of moral judgement as occurring in three consecutive phases: pre-conventional, conventional and post-conventional morality. Each phase involves two developmental stages:

naïve moral realism,	pragmatic morality;
socially shared perspectives,	social system morality;
human rights and social welfare morality, and	universal moral principles.

For example, at stage one the right action is one which helps avoid punishment, at stage two it is that which maximizes the reward, while at stage three the right action is one that brings the approval of others. Kohlberg's methodology of developing the capability to make moral judgements is based on finding solutions to moral dilemmas. For example, the teacher might ask a student who has difficulties in socialising to analyse the consequences of helping or refusing to help one of his or her classmate who is in trouble. The most effective technique is the analysis of moral implications, which takes place one stage higher than the actual level of a students' moral reasoning (Nucci, 1987). Thus if the determining factor in a student's moral decision is only the fear of punishment, it is appropriate to move the reasoning about pros and cons of particular action to the level of pragmatic morality, where the consequences of behaviour are analysed in terms of utility for him or his partners.

Another opportunity for developing students' decision-making in social interactions is through stimulating them to analyse the values that underlie their decisions (Good and Brophy, 1995). This is achieved by teaching students to identify the issue or describe the problem, to identify relevant facts and solutions, to project the probable consequences of alternative solutions, to arrive at a value decision, and finally to test and justify the decision. This justification is accomplished by showing how the decision meets four tests: role exchangeability (*would the student exchange their position with the person most disadvantaged by the decision?*); generality of consequences (*are the consequences of the decisions acceptable independently of the actor?*); transferability to new cases (*would the consequences apply if the decision was applied to a similar new situation?*); and subsumption (*is the justifying principle derived from a higher moral or value principle?*) (Good and Brophy, 1995, pp. 114–115).

Social learning theory

This approach synthesises behaviouralism and cognitive theories of learning, describing the acquisition of social skills through imitating models. It claims that a major part of social behaviour patterns are learned from single observations of a model, without any outside reinforcement. Often a form of immediate association appears between the model behaviour and the observer's cognitive – affective condition. As Gage and Berliner (1998) have pointed out, an act of social learning consists in remembering sensory events or visual coding of the model's conditions (and emotions) and in generalising the observed behaviours. When students later perceive that they are in a similar cognitive-affective condition, or perceive similar patterns of behaviour to those previously observed, these sensory events serve as cues to stimulate a similar reaction. Usually the social learning is spontaneous. However, if one wishes to intentionally stimulate learning of certain behavioural patterns, appropriate conditions can be provided. Bandura (1977, 1986) has shown that the acquisition of model behaviour involves four phases: attention, retention, reproduction, and motivation. Thus if we want a student to imitate certain behaviour, we should start from providing the conditions for effectively perceiving it. Secondly, measures should be taken to help a student to remember the appropriate behavioural pattern that is needed. Thirdly, if the target behaviour is complex, training should continue until a satisfactory level of performance is achieved. Fourthly, a positive attitude should be developed to apply this behavioural pattern in appropriate social conditions.

Creating favourable peer society

This is the most natural way for promoting social competence in immature students. However, this approach works only insofar as an isolated or rejected student retains the motivation for practising socialising with their peers. Consequently, special conditions should be arranged to provide students with practice in social interactions that are within their power, and that lead them to feelings of adequacy and increasing self-confidence.

Erwin (1993) suggests that at least three types of peer-assisted intervention programmes are possible: co-operative learning programmes, arranged interactions with peers, and arranged interactions with younger pupils.

Cooperative learning approaches use different task structures – such as working on independent tasks, or on interdependent tasks, or on the same task producing single product (McCaslin and Good, 1996). Of course, for the social development of students the two last examples deserve the most attention. Slavin found that group work approaches, where students are responsible for the mastery of the lesson by each student in the group, or where the achievement of the lesson objectives depends on the personal contribution of each student, have positive effects on intergroup relations (Slavin, 1994, p. 11). Also, a study by Sherif *et al.* (1961) showed that social relations between individual students and student groups can be improved by making them work jointly on some vitally important tasks.

Arranged interaction with peers and younger students. These approaches have a special focus on selecting partners to provide socially rejected students with successful socialising experiences. Erwin's survey of many studies suggested that attempts to improve the social standing of isolated children by manipulating their peer interactions did not give lasting effects. For example, partnering a child with low sociometric status with a more popular peer so that others observe their smooth interaction in organised cooperative group activities gave only a temporary effect (Erwin, 1993). Instead, partnering a socially less competent child with a younger child or children is more effective. For example, in school conditions a socially rejected but academically successful student could be made the peer tutor of a younger student. This experience of social interaction could help develop the isolated student's social skills and also increase his or her self-confidence in establishing social contacts (see Cohen, Kulik and Kulik, 1982).

Summary

Social competence is a major component of human practical intelligence. The formation of social skills and friendship relationships is laid down in early childhood. A basic layer of these skills is emotional adjustment, which Erikson explains as the solving of psychosocial crises. In later development, the affective aspect of social behaviour is supplemented by cognitive and psychomotor components of capabilities. In the emotional development of small children, the caregivers' parenting style plays the key role. The best preconditions for social development, including readiness for social interactions, are provided if parental love is combined with moderate restrictiveness. In school education it is a common problem that teachers discover difficulties students have in their social development belatedly, when the behavioural patterns are already deeply ingrained. The identification of these, and developing an adequate reaction to social immaturity, calls for knowledge of normal social development, recognition of abnormalities in this, and of what to do when corrections are needed. This chapter has analysed the development of social skills as the formation of empathetic and attribution capabilities and an understanding of friendship. The findings of this analysis are summarised in Damon's model of the development of the friendship relation. Sociometric methods and assessment by social partners are considered useful tools for the assessment of student social status and competence. Different intervention methods have been suggested for removing deficiencies in the development of social competence of students. These methods are based on behaviouristic, cognitive and neo-behaviouristic principles of learning, and are effective primarily for helping develop the components of social competence where these are lacking. The integral development of social competence can be secured by creating a controlled environment of social interaction, in which socially immature students experience feelings of self-effectiveness in socialising.

6

Early Childhood Eduction:
a meeting place for challenges

Ingrid Pramling Samuelsson and Anette Emilson

When children begin preschool as a first step in education (which in Sweden is from the ages of one to five), they enter a system built on the idea of mixing features from the home, the Kindergarten and the school. Three different settings, each with different views of and intentions for children. When they begin preschool the children also take their own personal experiences into a collective arena which already has societal intentions for them. At this crossroads of the single child and the group, challenges arise for further growth and learning. This itself is not a smooth process. It is a process related to the child's earlier experiences, to the child's level of social development and to the teachers' skills and knowledge in supporting the child. How the child will be included or excluded in the community of learners will make a difference for the child's future. In this chapter we will discuss children's social development and what current research tells about this, and also the critical question of what it means to be an individual in a collective preschool. Last but not least, we will discuss what preschool can do to prepare children for the global society.

Starting preschool

When Fröbel first developed the concept of the Kindergarten, the home and the mother constituted the basis of creating a good place for children to learn and develop. Household chores and gardening were the key factors in the construction of the daily programme (Fröbel, 1995), apart from the additions of mathematics and moral questioning. Kindergarten was not to be like school, but was to be a place where children's work, play and learning were laid out, as the three pillars of the Fröbel tradition.

Different preschool approaches have since emerged and taken the place of each other. However, most of these approaches have a common focus on the whole child, stressing that children's interests and experiences are important, as well as emphasising play in any form (Pramling Samuelsson and Asplund Carlsson, 2003). In consequence, it is the process or the 'how aspect' of learning that is central to early years education. The 'what aspect' – the content – is very much taken for granted. The simple situation of being an individual in a group of children has been viewed as a sufficient prerequisite for learning. This viewpoint means that children's social development and learning have always been considered as the main benefit of taking part in early education (Katz and McClellan, 1997).

The young child is mainly regarded by the family as an individual with different and specific needs. Caring is central (Halldén, 2001). Care also became a key factor in preschool, but care was also viewed as a prerequisite for learning and for the process of becoming social. It was at the move to the next step in the education system – to school – that care became subordinated to learning. At school, the focus became knowledge and facts that children should grasp – the 'what aspect' (SOU 1985: 22), and children were expected to have already developed the necessary social skills for taking part in school. Each of these three steps, from a caring family, to a preschool with focus on play and social development, to finally reaching school and being ready for cognitive learning, are integrated in the life-long learning perspective that is today argued for in most early childhood education curricula (Alvestad and Pramling Samuelsson, 1999; Karlsson-Lohmander and Pramling Samuelsson, 2002). Teachers today have had to come to terms with these earlier theories of child development and the notion of maturity. They have also had to make sense of socio-cultural theories, in which experience, communication, participation and the view of the competent child constitute the focus (Säljö, 2000; Sommer, 1997; Pramling Samuelsson and Asplund Carlsson, 2003).

As well as this theoretical perspective of learning in the early years, teachers also have to deal with the conflict between the individual child and the group of children. Throughout the day many situations occur in which individual interests, wishes and needs are confronted by the needs, wishes and interests of the group. This is an inevitable ethical dilemma for the teacher: to decide when, and on what grounds, to accept the group's wishes before the individual's and vice versa (Johansson, 2002, 2003; Johansson and Pramling Samuelsson, 2002). Although this relationship between the individual child and the group could be a dilemma, both the Swedish curriculum and new research (Ministry of Education and Science in Sweden, 1998a; Williams, 2001; Williams, Sheridan and Pramling Samuelsson, 2001; Johansson, 1999) support the importance of shared learning, not least the shared learning of values. In this way, common learning can become a resource for the individual child. It is important for all children that, from the early years, they become partners in a community of learners (Dalli, 1999; Rogoff, 1990; Smith, 1986). Young children also need to show the importance of the 'play world' that they create together with their peers, and that they also hold ethical values which they will defend from encroachment by other children (Johansson, 1999). The preschool has to simultaneously support and challenge every single child, since the intentions of society (expressed through the curriculum) are just as important as the individual experience of each child. This means that in preschool we cannot only focus on the act – the process – but must also ensure that the object – the content – is made explicit (Pramling Samuelsson and Asplund Carlsson, 2003).

Some aspects about social development in early years

Lilian Katz (2001) points to evidence accumulated over 25 years that unless a child achieves minimal social competence by about the age of six, plus or minus a half year, the child is at risk for the rest of his or her life (see also Katz and McClellan, 1997; Ladd and Burgess, 1999; Coplan *et al.*, 2000).

Research into the functioning of the brain shows that a child is pattern-seeking rather than pattern-receiving (Rutter and Rutter, 1992). The very first year of life gives the child the experience of interaction between themselves and others (Trevarthen, 1992). This pattern-seeking behaviour means that whatever social skills the child has developed before entering preschool, the likelihood is that others will react to the child in a way that reinforces the pattern of the child's reaction. If a child is friendly and approachable, others will welcome his or her company, and engage and interact with the child. These acts will help the child gain confidence as a social participant. In interaction with others, the child will polish their pre-existing skills and acquire new ones. Following Katz (*op cit.*), the child who is easy to like will in this way become more likeable, in a positive recursive cycle. Of course, this also works in the opposite way for a child who is lacking these early positive social skills. He or she will go into a negative cycle in their social interactions, unless we act and react as teachers (see Krull, chapter 6).

We now know a great deal about what kind of help we can offer these children. Prerequisites for being social and becoming able to interact with other children are communicative skills and competencies, which are closely related to wider issues of language development. Communicative competence arises from conversation and interaction with other children and adults. Young children are more likely to communicate in smaller groups than in large groups, and when they find communication meaningful and enjoyable. Play is one of these key activities, but there are also other experiences in which children feel they are participants and which will enhance communication skills. As Katz (2001, p. 7) says: 'There must be something to talk about! Something that matters to the talkers: something of interest and significance to them.' Of course, the teachers' skills and competence are major factors for creating such a high quality environment, but structural factors are also of importance, such as the child/adult ratio and so on (Asplund Carlsson, Pramling Samuelsson and Kärrby, 2001), in giving support and in challenging the child's social development.

Inclusion and exclusion

It is every child's right to attend preschool in Sweden, and because of this the upbringing and socialisation of children and young people has increasingly become a concern of society (Persson, 2001). In this context socialisation may be understood as the process by which the individual acquires the current norms and structures of society, and by this process becomes part of society (Illeris, 2000). It is clear that questions concerning children's and young people's socialisation and their development of identity are on the contemporary social agenda. The current debate claims, among other things, that a child's understanding of society, its development of an identity and the formation of citizenship begins at birth and continues throughout all of life. The little child, from the beginning of life, appears as an active person and as a co-designer of his or her own identity, at the same time that he or she is recognised as a part of and a member of society (Dahlberg, Moss and Pence, 2002). The preschool, as one context among the many in which citizenship is exercised, has unique possibilities and a great responsibility for integrating all children in society. If children are socially included from the beginning of preschool we need not talk about integration. The preschool is intended to be a place for social encounters for boys and girls, for those from different cultures and social groups, and for children in need of special support. It is here that children are supposed to become able to – among other things – grow into independent human beings who respect and have consideration for those who think differently from themselves (Skolverket, 2000).

Preschool for everyone can be seen both as a didactic challenge and as a goal emphasised in the curriculum. In a recently published research review of theses on child pedagogy over two decades (1980–1999) Klerfelt (2000) praises Swedish child care for living up to the intention of preschooling for all. However, Klerfelt is also of the opinion that there has been a recent change in the ideological debate: words like *democracy*, *solidarity* and *fellowship* have been exchanged for market-oriented terms of *efficiency* and *cost-consciousness*, which could suggest that the intention of preschool for all may be threatened. Peder Haug in Norway (1998) considers that in society today it is possible to discern a distinct tendency towards segregation, with a consequent risk of marginalisation.

An integrative and inclusive pedagogy, with the best of intentions, can, in different circumstances, become instead a segregating pedagogy. Consequently Haug makes a distinction between 'segregating integration' and 'inclusive integration'. In preschool, 'segregating integration' implies that children from different cultures or social groups, or children in need of special support, attend the same group but that those who, for one reason or another, prove to be in a complicated social situation are separated or segregated from the fellowship of the group. According to Haug, 'segregating integration' has as its starting point the concept of deficiencies within the child, in which the reasons for the problems are perceived as biological rather than sociological, that is, they are more connected to nature than to culture. An approach such as this may, according to Qvarsell (2001), be regarded as a remnant of a psychological and medical perspective focused on the needs of children. This is an approach which for a long time has dominated research on children and which has strongly influenced the way of viewing children and the attitude towards children in pedagogical practice. Further, Dahlberg, Moss and Pence (2002) suggest that the tradition of developmental psychology that is connected to preschooling functions as a technology for normalisation, that determines how a child should be. This creates a hierarchy among children, in which their position depends on whether or not the child has reached a specific 'normal' stage of development. Dahlberg *et al.* report that this results in a focus on attempting to reach the norm, and on pre-cluding or correcting divergence from the norm. An example of this kind of normalising discourse in pedagogic practice would be the classification of disadvantaged children who are at risk, or of children with special needs, both of which are the subject of special attention in many countries (*op cit*). Differentiating particular children as being more in need than others is intended to ensure that children's different prerequisites are met. While such differentia-tion can mean adjusting an activity within the framework of an inclusive pedagogy, it can also mean that the children who are identified in this way are placed in different groups or activities, on the basis of an estimation of their possibility of managing the demands of the activity (Persson, 2001). Haug (1998) is critical of such segregation as a starting point, arguing that this expresses the view that it is the children who are supposed to 'be adjusted' to the instrumental environment, rather than vice versa.

However, in an integrated inclusive preschool all children partici-pate actively in all activities on the basis of their own ability and skills. Such inclusion is based on democratic participation, equal value and social justice, according to Haug. Persson (*op. cit.*) reports that this use of the expression 'inclusive' was coined in the USA in the late 1980s, and that it implies that there are demands on the whole educational system and the whole of society to constantly and actively adjust practice so that all children and young people feel that they participate meaningfully in pedagogic practice, so that no one is excluded from the community of learners. This discussion thus starts from the premise that the best and most impartial prac-tice, for each individual and for society, is that everyone – irrespec-tive of qualifications, interests and performance – meet together in an activity. Through this are created the conditions for a community in a broader context. In an inclusive practice, great importance is laid on social training and on the development of a community – not by searching for similarities between people, but by affirming differences. By accepting that there are differences between

children, differences should become part of daily experience, form-
ing the basis for an individualising practice. The encounter between
the individual and the collective is complex, but in this context is
understood as individually oriented activity *within* the collective.
This means that all children are accepted on the basis of their
qualifications and possibilities, but that this is done within the context of the community. The activities of the preschool must therefore be adjusted to each child, and must rest on the basis of the
common values of a society, irrespective of individual background
(Ministry of Education and Science in Sweden, 1998a). In this way,
Haug suggests (1998), individualisation becomes a condition for an
inclusive integration.

A pedagogical activity that starts from such a basis of differences
will affirm heterogeneity and lack of likeness, in preference to
valuing unity and homogeneity. According to Carl-Anders
Säfström (2002), such grounds for socialisation and for the creation
of identity implies dislocation from the process of capturing someone into the system, the person already identified as an outsider, to
respect the same individual for what he or she is. To achieve this it
is necessary to invite an encounter with 'the other'. If we wish to
know who 'the other' is, we have to meet each other. In her thesis
Vad eller Vem ('What or Who') Moira von Wright (2000) stresses
the importance of inter-subjectivity for pedagogic practise. By this,
she means that when we wish to understand both ourselves and
each other, pedagogic practice should be permeated by a relational
perspective, which sets out from concrete inter-human relations.
What then becomes essential are the actions of individuals and the
processes of interaction – situations of interaction in which children
and adults meet in communication. This inter-subjective encounter
includes simultaneous understanding that demands the complete
presence and attention of the pedagogue. These encounters may be
of particular significance to small children in preschool, since an
inter-subjective encounter holds the possibility for those involved
mutually to share reality.

How can this be expressed in practice? How can it be done with the youngest children, who have not yet developed a verbal language? Gunvor Løkken (2000) bases her research on this on the theory of Merleau-Ponty, which – in a similar line of argument to that used above – implies that the condition for understanding other people is in the meeting or the interaction with them. Løkken emphasises how the young child understands the world through the body. The body is the point of departure in the world, and language is incorporated in the gestures of the body. Bodily communication is thus equivalent to verbal communication. The child's message, shown in songs, dancing, playing and creating, is consequently, in this context, equally seriously in meaning as is an adult's expressions in conversation and in writing (Barnombudsmannen [Children's Ombudsman], 2000). The pedagogic consequence of this is that an adult in the preschool must learn to interpret and understand children's expressions, so that the young child can be taken seriously and be included in its own pedagogical context. It is also essential to create the best conditions for the child to be able to express itself in the preschool. Young children have opinions and, according to the Barnombudsmannen (2000), it is the responsibility of adults to develop ways to give even the youngest children the opportunity to make themselves heard and listened to.

One conclusion that can be draw from this line of argument is that the inclusion or exclusion of children in their pedagogical context, as well as in society, is on the whole the responsibility of adults.

Early learning for a global society

Each adult views the world in relation to his/her norms and values, whether they are aware of it or not. Young children develop or take in values through their experiences in everyday life, as well as from other people. Children's experience and awareness with their bodies becomes a basis for the future. What do we want the next generation to learn then?

The Swedish curriculum for preschool (Ministry of Education and Science in Sweden, 1998a, p. 6) states:

An important task of the preschool is to establish and help children acquire the values on which our society is based. The inviolability of human life, individual freedom and integrity, the equal value of all people, equality between the genders as well as solidarity with the weak and vulnerable are all values that the school shall actively promote in its work with children.

In the curriculum for schools (Ministry of Education and Science in Sweden, 1998b) it says, among other things, that the school should strive to ensure that all pupils:

- have knowledge about the interdependence of countries and different parts of the world, and

- know the requirements for a good environment and understand basic ecological contexts.

These statements could be summarized as 'global understanding'. Young children are expected to eventually complete school that we all live in a global society, in which we are all dependent on each other. This includes the basic values necessary for participating in and working for a democratic and fair world – something which brings many demands to develop different qualities in children. There are already a great many common intentions within Europe. Notions such as joy, freedom, spontaneity, communication, symbolism, engagement, sociality, means (instruments, resources) dominate these goals – the process is more important than the product (Council for Cultural Co-operation, 1996).

Children already live in a global society, in which international agreements are signed about children's rights (for example, the United Nations Convention on the Rights of the Child, 1989). The world also exists in children's everyday life, not only through the media and toys, but also through the multicultural settings many children encounter in their preschool (Pramling Samuelsson, 2002 a, b).

The child's right to participate is not a matter of course, or an indisputable paragraph in the Convention. Eva Johansson (1999) shows in her study how children between the ages of one and three will fight for their rights in preschool. They fight for their rights to objects and to share space with other children. In preschool all objects (toys, materials, and so on) belong to everybody, and this is something which children perceive very soon when they start preschool. What also seems to be the code in preschool is that the one who is using an object has the current right to this object, but conflicts appear when one child's right is confronted with other child's rights. For example, when a child leaves 'his' toy car for a moment, he may still regards it as 'his', but at the same time as another child may thinks that he can now use it, since nobody else is using it. How do adults deal with such conflicts? Often they ask: 'Who was using the toy first', a value we might question if it was always asked. Young children seem to have an intuitive feeling for rights. Young children seem to consider the owner to have an unquestioned right to personal belongings, that is, that the right of the owner is superior to the right to use an object. Existing norms, according to Johansson, seem to be:

- *control*, that is, the one who actively uses something has the right,

- *time*, that is, being first give a right to the object, and

- *strength*, that is, if you possess physical or psychical strength, you can exercise your right.

This means that very young children's acting and interplay – with other children as well as with adults in preschool – forms the foundation of the children's norms and values. Children's play in preschool becomes part of their existence and identity, in the formation of their own rights and of their shared rights in a collective. When individual and shared rights meet, the understanding grows stronger, and it is here that adults are needed – specifically, adults who have considered which values are important to support the goals and intentions stated in the curriculum. But when children are concerned and actively involved, they will interact and fight for their own rights!

Another aspect of the global society with consequences for our survival is the environment – 'the sustainable society'. This is also a content which could be introduced early to the very young child, for them to gradually develop a deeper and more complex understanding over time (Sjøberg, 2000). At a first glance this might be seen as natural science, but in praxis it is related to justice and democracy. Working towards a global understanding means developing values and knowledge that are related to the child's immediate surroundings, their everyday experience, and how his or her experience must constitute the basis, every day and in every situation.

In the complex learning environment of the preschool, the individual child, other children and the teachers are all participants. The context of learning is partly learning as such (Säljö, 2000). But for young children approaches to learning and to content are interwoven, so that the object of learning (what his/her awareness is directed towards) becomes as important as the act (how the learning is shaped and conducted) (Pramling Samuelsson and Asplund Carlsson, 2003). This means that when the teacher works on developing a global content, young children must meet the values the teacher wants to foster and that the teacher must draw attention to communication and reflection. Here the fundamental keys are both the child's perspective (Doverborg and Pramling Samuelsson, 2000) and the teacher's support and challenges.

To develop citizenship in Europe means both to work on certain contents such as values, and also to relate to each child in an appropriate way for his or her learning and growth. The consequence of this perspective on learning is that one cannot start by developing the child's social competence and then afterwards continue by developing an understanding of different aspects of the world – one has to work simultaneously on the child's total development, socially, emotionally and intellectually. The tools for supporting and challenging this are relations and communications with peers and adults, and the child's own sense of security in his or her identity. It is here the teacher's awareness, knowledge and skills become a matter of vital importance for how and if early childhood education will become a meeting place for challenges or not!

7

Who is afraid of social learning?

Hugo Verkest

There were too many eyes and ears controlling us during our project on waste (teacher, age 38)

For some children the experience of TV is their only source of knowledge (teacher, age 28)

While visiting student teachers undertaking professional placements in schools, we collected data about work in schools on controversial social issues. For example, after the events of September 11, 2001 we interviewed teachers about their children's behaviour and practice. The teachers' fundamental question to us was 'How can we handle the fear we see in the eyes of our children?' followed by 'How can we critically select visual information?' This provided an opportunity to think about strategies to work with 'hot issues' in social learning (Verkest, 2002).

Many school boards and administrators still think that anything related to learning about values as a political hot potato, which is consequently to be avoided. They need many examples and success stories showing how schools have approached this in ways that have not been controversial and that have had some measure of success (Lickona, 1991).

If we want to engage in social education we will have to analyse the images and the 'visual' world in which the children now live. There is a growing concern about society's moral and spiritual condition, which can be seen in various trends in young people's behaviour: the rise in youth violence; increasing dishonesty; the growing disrespect for parents, teachers, and other authority figures; an increase in bigotry and crimes related to racism and xenophobia; the deterioration of language; a rise in instances of self-destructive behaviour; a decline in personal and civic responsibility, all of which might be included under the term 'ethical illiteracy' (Lickona, 1991; Turnbaugh-Lockwood 1997).

The power of mass media

A recent Belgian research project pointed to a significant relationship between watching commercial television and intolerance, insecurity and aggression. Many of the extreme right voters in Flanders watch commercial television: broadcasts (including radio) provide less knowledge and enrichment and more diversion and escape. These programmes influence the viewer – they provide fun and amusement, but while viewers become emotionally engaged they do not become particularly interested observers of society (Hooghe, 2002).

Some of the answers given to the researchers could be categorised as 'television answers' rather than 'real world answers'. One question was about whether most fatal violence happened between strangers (the television answer) or between relatives or acquaintances (a real-world view). Heavy television viewers (those who said they watched television or video for four or more hours a day) were more likely to be more fearful of violence than light viewers (those watching less than two hours a day).

The rise of mass media is one of the most important social evolutions of recent decades. Coupled with the ageing population and with the increasing social exclusion of semi and unskilled workers in our knowledge-based society, this contributes to an impression of general malaise and dysfunctional society (Elchardus and Smits, 2002).

The lack of power of the masses

The need to develop more social education in Flanders is linked closely to the increasing complexity of social life and the feeling many people have of being less in control of their lives and a sense of lack of access. A general malaise, which started in the eighties, is described in social studies, and in novels and literature (Lanoye, 2002). A keyword is *uncomfortable*: since the *affaire* Dutroux (concerning missing, abused and murdered children) there is less and less trust in our social and political institutions (Huyse, 1994). This discomfort is seen in people's gloomy perspectives and those lacking in social perspective are largely intolerant and sceptical about democratic institutions: little wonder that people have this unease and prefer the content of commercial television.

A new curriculum: a challenge and an opportunity

In the late nineties a new curriculum subject was introduced for schools in Flanders, under the title of 'world orientation' (1998), which can be seen as one particular educational response to the political malaise described above. Those designing this subject tried to link a series of different dimensions within a holistic approach and innovatively moved pupils away from facts that had to be learned by heart. This new curriculum subject required teachers to work in a more interactive manner and to look for fundamental issues (VVKBO, 1998). But was this really an innovation?

The curriculum that had been introduced in 1936 was a landmark, as well as a precursor for 'world orientation', proposing that children's work focus on centres of interest in second level education and village schools. It recommended subjects such as the brook, the street, the bus, the railway, the post office, the fire station, the smith (and other traditional professions): in general the focus was on nature and social behaviour rather than on culture and goods. This curriculum required teachers to bring children into contact with nature, goods and their practical consequences, and to study the immediate environment. The accent on physical geography may also have had something to do with the influence of the French tradition (the most important designer of this curriculum, Jeunehomme, was Walloon by birth) and of the Belgian school innovator Decroly, who had had a scientific education. In Decroly's vision knowledge was derived from the natural environment and, to a lesser degree, the social environment, in which humans have to meet their basic needs (of food, living, working, protection against disease and danger). This environment was considered to be static: the individual was expected to adapt himself or herself to society, and society was not to be criticised or changed (Feys, 1998).

We also found a more transcendental approach in our research on the educational heritage (in more than 300 articles) of Hector Defoort (1878–1940). A West-Flemish headteacher, he was considered an important exponent of a new way of pedagogical thinking in the period between the World Wars. (Verkest, 2003). By means of songs, poems, short stories, pictures, theatre and text books Defoort stimulated the 'apperception' (conscious perception) and the 'interest' of children and teachers. The theory of these two principles had already been introduced in the first Flemish Pedagogical Scientific Journal (Van Langendonck, 1922). Defoort left the traditional deductive path, that had been so typical of Catholic ways of teaching, and advocated a more inductive approach. Van Langendonck had introduced the idea of 'capital' – prior knowledge of social issues held by children. Defoort adapted this idea through the practice of formulating open questions, giving time for observation in class, telling stories and organising excursions in nature (such as visits to the river, greenhouse, or farm) holding that these would stimulate the children's wondering about experiences linked to God's creation. All the issues of 'world orientation' promoted the children's moral and spiritual life (Verkest and Heus, 2003).

Raf Feys analysed the school subjects studied by students in teacher training college since 1971, evaluating both handbooks and curricula description. He concluded that the approach to world orientation was particularly one-sided and related mainly to physical characteristics. During a recent observation of a student's teaching practice the following subjects were covered: spring, pigs, the sowing season, the parts of a plant, the use of water, rabbits, cows, onions, the clock, rivers and streams, and the times of Charles the Great (Feys, 1998).

Attention used to be paid in progressive educational circles to the social aspects of world orientation and to thematic approaches. Since the 1970s progressive educators also tended to advocate projects concerning peace, the consequences of high levels of consumption, the environment, traffic, and so on. These will not be found explicitly in the curriculum schedules of specific educational subjects, but are generally found or implied within broader educational objectives.

Educators are now increasingly regarding world orientation as a valuable field for learning that is broader and much wider than the theoretical subjects of the curriculum, and one that is very open to study by children of all ages. Until the introduction of this new curriculum subject, third grade teaching in this area was dominated by three separate subjects (biology, geography and history) each of which was given an hour per week. Now 'world orientation' has this time, plus an additional hour.

Parents as new supporters of social learning

Teachers become discouraged if they feel that parents are indifferent to their efforts, but parents may sometimes feel that in areas of social learning school is stepping in and becoming a surrogate for the family, taking over what is properly the role and responsibility of parents. Schools must therefore develop strategies to actively involve parents. If they cannot get parents to come to the school to discuss their children's social development, they have to find ways to involve the parents through the child.

Children can, for example, report home on a values project in a 'class diary', or they might interview their parents about their

93

attitudes toward social problems such as waste or food. A number of successful programmes on issues such as sexual behaviour have involved sending copies of what was discussed in the day at school home to parents, to provide an opportunity for parents to continue the conversation with their child and add their own perspectives to what has been discussed in school. They have also been encouraged to give extra information and their point of view through the internet and email.

One of the greatest dangers facing social education is that severe social problems will only be met with a weak educational response. There are parents who, perhaps understandably, do not trust the schools to act responsibly in areas such as these.

The teacher as the third adult

It is possible to suggest that there are three categories of adults who relate to young people:

(1) loving and concerned parents, who want the very best for their children;

(2) the consumer society itself – not at all loving, but concerned to profit from the desires of the generation of young people and

(3) in between these two, a relatively rare third type of adult, often as loving (sometimes even more loving) than the parents themselves but not concerned with profit – for example, the reliable youth leader or the approachable teacher. They do not sell goods, and they simply offer values. Without such people, education is not possible – certainly not social initiation. These people take care of the world of the inner life – the internal bruisings and injuries, seeing how many of those in the first and second world (who may often sympathise with the third and the fourth world) are lonely deep inside – their outward commitments may have destroyed their inner warmth (Versteylen, 1991). Teacher and pupils can become each other's partners in dialogue, in which the central element is not the transfer of

knowledge but the interaction between learners and subject, not least making visible the teacher's own cultural background.

To do justice to this connection between the dialogue of the learners and the dialectics of core words and experiencing, the traditional didactic triangle of teacher, pupils and learning contents must be extended to a pedagogic didactic quadrangle – of the guide to learning (teacher), learner, core words, and experience (Schaap, 1984).

In such a dialogical teaching-learning situation, this learning dialogue is of primary concern, in which special attention must be paid to mutually open relationships, to the personal contribution of participants, to the question-and-answer structuring core words and to the skill needed to distinguish between core words.

Crucial in this is the existence of school culture that allows teachers to ask for help. In many schools, when the teacher asks for help this is seen as a deficiency, and very differently from a school in which it is accepted that all teachers need help and support. To have real democracy we need all children to do well in school. It is very short-sighted to imagine that we children only need to care for. Teachers cannot work effectively if they are frustrated by students mainstreamed into classes; and teachers will feel frustrated by being unable to give the time they see these children need, and by their own lack of preparation to meet these needs. They will need the same things as all teachers: support, time to share and resources. They will also need people to honour their questions and help them find answers, and the first question for teachers working on social learning is 'What do you need?' – to which the answer is planning time and trust.

Collaboratively taught classrooms can be the most wonderful, because there will be another set of eyes and of ears, and another brain. But teachers must calculate some of the following factors if this is not to be counter productive.

Take care of yourself! The 'emo(tional) factor' in social education

Sometimes teachers will be reluctant to engage in direct social education, because they worry that someone will object. Teachers need the security of a school-wide effort that will legitimate their efforts and give them strength.

Educators increasingly believe that without the most basic rules of decency, teaching and learning cannot take place. School directors and older teachers often maintain that increasing numbers of children are coming to school without fundamental values, without a minimal sense of right or wrong, and without basic trust. Schools know that if they do not do develop character, they will not be able to accomplish much else.

In one of the schools we visited, one teacher begins each school year by focusing on a value a week. He starts with caring. Gathering the children into a philosophical circle, he asks a series of questions around a doll. When do you need your dolly? Have you ever lost it? What kind of dolly do you have? Does the dolly care for you, or do you care for the dolly? Has your dolly a special place? Is it good to have a class dolly? How can each of us show caring in our classroom, our school, our neighbourhood and our families? So a new topic arises – security. This will be the highlighted value of the next week. The teacher then makes a visual map of all of the children's responses, and displays this at the front of the room. He will read a story or a fairy tale about caring, and start a discussion with the children. Subsequently, he looks for opportunities during the rest of the day to make connections between the discussion about caring and the children's personal behaviour.

If a child behaves in a caring way, he will compliment the child. If a child behaves in an uncaring or thoughtless way, he will privately – not in public – ask the child if that behaviour showed caring. Each day of the week he reads a different story or shows a video on caring and again sets up a discussion. By the end of the week, he says that caring has turned into flesh and blood. This is one of many ways to weave core values into the fabric of the classroom.

We are the world! The 'eco(logical) factor' in social learning

Within this project the concept of linking is an expression of concern for the development of positive orientations towards reality: it offers a point of reference for the value of education in general.

Linking with the ecosystem is essentially a religious concept. Etymologically, 're-ligion' (re-liare) means 'linking again', just as 'de-linquency' means 'the lack of being linked'. The basic sense of connectedness can be seen as a cornerstone that prevents criminal behaviour or action that damages things and people. In early childhood and in primary and secondary education children are helped to develop this attitude of linking with themselves, with others, with the material world, with society and with the ultimate unity of the eco–system (Cuvelier, 1998). This leads to the development of the concepts of involvement and well-being. The Leuven Research Centre in Belgium has developed a process-oriented child monitoring system that helps teachers identify children with socio-emotional problems and with special developmental needs. These are children who have not been successful in achieving a satisfactory interaction with their environment. They are pressured, and lose contact with their inner experiential stream (Laevers, 1997).

The eco-dimension of social education is now translated into 'sustainable development'. The World Commission on Environment and Development (WCED) describes sustainability as meeting 'the needs of the present without compromising the ability of future generations to meet their own needs'. This means that short-term aims and goals need to be connected with long-term perspectives (WCED, 1987). It is a challenge for teacher training institutions to translate this contemporary issue in pedagogical and didactic road maps. It is a policy topic still situated at the academic level, with little implementation at the level of professional practice (for example, in secondary and primary schools). The policy recognises inequity as the largest environmental problem in the world: no ecology without equity; no equity without ecology (WCED, 1987). Social education that incorporates the concept of sustainability will not be neutral and value-free.

Don't worry, be happy! The 'ethos factor' in social education.

Values such as respect, responsibility, honesty and fairness promote and affirm human dignity, supporting the development and welfare of the individual person. They clearly serve the common good, and meet the classical ethical test of reversibility: would you want to be treated in this way? They also meet the test of universalism: would you want all people to act this way in similar situations?

Social learning does not simply wait for teachable moments to arise: it creates teachable moments itself. It creates opportunities to teach, model, promote, and celebrate core ethical values.

The two threats to the moral health of any society occur firstly when many people do bad things, and secondly when many people do bad things and don't have a clue that what they are doing is wrong. There has been growing evidence of this sort of ethical illiteracy, especially among young people (Lickona, 1991; Turnbaugh-Lockwood, 1997).

A comprehensive approach would require the teacher to act as a caregiver, a model and a mentor, treating students with love and respect, supporting prosocial behaviour and correcting hurtful actions, and so on. Teachers should create a moral community, helping students to know and respect each other, and to feel valued in the group as a whole. Other principles in such an approach would include the practice of moral discipline, the creation of a democratic classroom environment, teaching values through the curriculum, using cooperative learning to develop students' appreciation of others, developing 'the conscience of craft' by fostering student's work ethic, developing the habit of moral reflection, and teaching conflict resolution. Such principles would make full use of the potential for moral life that is to be found in the classroom.

In mounting such a school wide effort, it would also be important to avoid ethical schizophrenia – where one thing is said in the classroom, and another is carried out in another parts of the school environment, such as the corridors, the school restaurant or the games field. Consistency is the business of ethical life.

Take a chance! The 'kairos factor' in social learning

In the last decade Flemish Belgium has had to deal with not only urban policy problems but also several rural policy issues: swinefever, dioxins in the food chain, overproduction of vegetables, overmanuring, family dramas and the murder of a famous veterinarian fighting against the hormone mafia. A long list of social catastrophes dominated our visual media. But at the same time there were several more positive projects, of agricultural organisations, of alternative environmental movements and the government initiative to promote rural development and project a positive image through new projects. These could be seen to focus around such keywords as quality, justice and sustainable development. At school, children have the same questions as their parents about the security of their food. Several schools organised projects about health, food, rural activities and waste. Some of these worked through the method of 'see – judge – act', and others through the basic questions of 'what do I already know?' and 'what would I like to know?' The Greek word *kairos* is used to symbolise both a decisive option and at the same time the opportunity to strengthen the struggle for justice. *Kairos* is the opposite of crisis. In this, the action dimension is not purely instrumental, and human decisions are not just technically rational. It is not enough to raise children in a fire brigade ethic to argue in favour of fire extinguishers.

The application of such participatory methods to create new environments for children is complicated by several factors, including the traditional typical roles that adults or teachers play in a child's life. Our evaluations found that teachers were adamant that collaboration in a school project on topics such as waste and food security was very difficult. They were not unhappy at tackling these topics, but argued that if the projects were to have any intellectual depth, it would take more a few meetings and a bottle of water (in recyclable bottles) to accomplish something worthwhile. *'You really have to work to understand the different points of view, and then you have to try to carefully involve the meaning of those different points of view as they are woven together into something better'*, was one comment by a teacher involved in the project on waste.

Collaboration deepens and enriches the work, but it also requires a kind of scholarly commitment, which many do not understand. To put this another way: collaboration is not simply adding things together – it is reconceptualising the whole basis of an experience in a different form.

Get the picture! The 'visual factor' in social education!

In most of the projects we examined teachers used a lot of visual data. In relation to learning, the use of two-dimensional and three-dimensional images offered three major advantages. Firstly, they are highly *memorable*. Like songs, pictures stick in the head. Secondly, they are highly *motivating*, particularly so for children, adolescents, and young adult learners. Images in their many forms constitute a powerful subculture, and it would be unwise to ignore this flexible and attractive resource. Indeed, history, civic education and religious education have always made good use of images. Anything that can be done with a text can be done with a picture. Thirdly, using 2-D and 3-D data gets children on the same wavelength and creates *common goals, targets and terminology,* and makes formal modelling much easier, faster and more accurate. Concepts such as identity and sense of public responsibility can be visualised in this way. Using games and cartoons can create various environments and instruments that facilitate global discussion and dialogue (Vandemaele, 2002).

People generally enjoy cartoons, and they can be seen as fun and helpful when used to explain difficult ideas. They are easy to relate to, and cartoon art is a powerful way to talk about difficult and scary issues. Some educators fail to recognise the validity of visual learning, believing that it leads to a lower quality of thinking, or is something that less intelligent people may resort to – a prejudice that cannot be sustained given the weight of available evidence.

Cartoons can be a guide for young people and an entertainment for adults. A cartoon has forcible language. It is not always an harmonious relationship between the artist and society.

> Cartoonists brought – and bring – the ups and downs of the world in the second part of the century so sharp, mocking, unmasking because undoubtedly choosing for the poor, the weak, the oppressed, the exploited in pictures. These artists gave the people a visual memory. They offer a wealth of portraits of an era that can be passed on to our children. Their very reason of existence as cartoonists involves raising their voices when the conventional journalists get silent. Political cartoonists ask their 'readers' to follow current news. One has to know the relationships and has to know who is doing what to whom. The work of a cartoonist is an emanation of a mental process and not of a spontaneous explosion. (Verkest, 2001)

Conclusion

We referred above to our research on pedagogical thinking during (in) the inter-war period. Some Flemish-Catholic educators (Decoene, Le Hovre and Langendonck) introduced the slogan *'Nova et Vetera'* ('New and old') in 1922. This meant that social education can be characterised as *vetera* (old) if the pupil has sufficient pre-existing knowledge to clearly understand it, while education can be characterised as *nova* either if it improves the pupil's pre-existing knowledge or if it uses this knowledge to fit with new information.

The 'school-wide factors for social learning' that have been derived in this article may be implemented in such a strategy: fostering care beyond the classroom, using positive role models to inspire unselfish altruism, and providing opportunities at all levels in school and community service.

We suggest creating a total moral environment or ethos, which is supported by values taught in class. This implies the leadership from the principal, a whole school plan for discipline, the creation of a moral community among adults, and putting a priority on moral concerns, without which effective moral education is impossible (Turnbaugh-Lockwood, 1997).

The practice described here, based on the new Flanders curriculum, shows a holistic and personalised alternative to the positivistic approaches of the past (Janssens, 1999). Teacher and children are no longer viewed as incapable of jointly determining the content of their own education, of setting their own goals and objectives that are compatible with the community they live in.

With Lodewijks-Frencken (1995), we believe that creating time in which to reflect on moral and social concerns at school is essential. Too frequently other matters – such as daily crises – receive most attention from school staff. Teachers need to be allowed to evaluate their own teaching and learning without fear. In this context we should recall the wisdom of John Donne 'No man is an island entire of itself; every man is a piece of the continent'.

8

Youth and society in France: between common conceptions and school knowledge

Nicole Tutiaux-Guillon and Jane Mejias

Schooling is explicitly intended to educate young people to be responsible and efficient, by giving them the knowledge thought necessary to act in real life. This objective is used to socially legitimise many of the subjects taught to teenagers. Does school effectively attain this objective?

'Social facts' may be principally defined to distinguish the social from the individual. Emile Durkheim characterises social facts as both external and constraining. They are external to the individual, because they both pre-exist him or her, and will continue to exist after his or her death. They are constraining, because they impose rules and penalties. But these rules are generally internalised, and thus become unnoticed or, so to speak, 'natural'. Any sufficiently regularly occurring collective aspect of human reality is a social fact; but this definition is too broad for our present analysis, particularly because it refers to political, economical and cultural facts as social. We have therefore used a more restrictive approach, emphasising the structure of society and collective relationships. Even so, a larger field could have been explored, including, for example, urban problems or sociability. We have decided to limit our analysis firstly to data from research on how young people between 15 and 18 years old understand some social facts, secondly to confine our study to those topics which correspond to what is taught in secondary school, through history, economics and social studies: family, work, social cohesion, and social structure.

Firstly, we examine young people's conceptions of these facts. We have taken data from several different enquiries (surveys, qualitative analysis, empirical studies) among 15 to 18 year old students. Some of these topics were the subject of direct enquiry, and some were developed as ideas by young people in the course of interview. All these studies show the importance of values, idealism and personal experience in shared conceptions of society.

Secondly, we question the impact of what is taught in school, separating arbitrarily three types of relationships between what is taught and what is believed to be 'true' by the students.

This structure reflects our main question: if school is intended to train young people to be responsible and efficient in real life, does it succeed in this? And if it does not, why not?

Young people's understanding of social facts

As a rule, young people's ability to talk about society is limited: they have no abstract frame of thought to describe or analyse it. In a 1997 study, 106 students (aged 14 or 15) were asked to 'give three to five words that would be useful to describe or to understand a society'. Only five per cent of the sample suggested words such as 'social class' or 'culture'; only one per cent put forward words or phrases such as 'standard of living', 'bourgeoisie', 'way of life' and so on. Almost 25 per cent did not know the meaning of 'society'. A parallel questionnaire was given to older students who were 17 years old: the responses were only a little higher, mainly where students had attended a course of economics and social studies. In another study, on the teaching and learning of social history, about forty 14 to 18 years old students were interviewed (Tutiaux-Guillon, 2000a). In their responses these teenagers often lacked the specific vocabulary needed to talk about society. The words they most commonly employed – 'standard of living', 'way of life – were given rather vague or commonplace meanings, as in the example 'the capitalist society, that's, if you want something, you have to sort it out of yourself' [all of these student quotations are our translation]. Most words, although they had been introduced in the lessons, were either used incorrectly or not used at all. For example, 60 per cent of the students interviewed did not use the words 'social class'; of those who did use it, 66 per cent saw the main idea of the concept was a difference in wealth, and for 50 per cent it conveyed an idea of power or subjection. For most of the interviewees, when the economic gap between classes is reduced, class itself just disappears: some said bluntly 'in our society there are no more social classes'. Students' use of vocabulary is thus not a reliable index for assessing their level of understanding. Surveys in which students are offered different propositions, and then asked to take their own position, can give us a more precise indication of their knowledge of social facts.

There is no French specific research on how young people understand social facts and problems, as there is for politics. But research about teaching and learning social sciences, focussed on certain subjects – work, past societies, and comparison with present-day society, Europe – give significant findings about what young people believe and what they learn. The following four detailed examples explore this further.

Family: children's conception

Family is an important value, which is largely approved of, irrespective of age, social or cultural background. In the *Youth and History* survey, 87 per cent of French teenagers said the family was of 'very great' or 'great' importance and 67 per cent indicated that their family history was of great or very great interest to them. A qualitative analysis using data from collective interviews with groups of students aged 15 to 18, and from using Q-sort[1] analysis in the classroom indicated that teenagers regard the family as a warm refuge from the difficulties of economic life. But this refuge is more of a wish than a reality, and depends largely on the family's social situation and its financial resources (Bloss, 1996). In the interviews conducted by Tutiaux-Guillon (2000a), some students spoke about *the* family or about their family: their emphasis was often on solidarity between parents and children, or even on parents' devotion to their children.

At the same time, a very large proportion of young people perceive the family as an institution in crisis. The signs are obvious to them: the drop in fecundity rates, the fragility of relationships, and the crisis of marriage as an institution. These perceptions do not always coincide with the observations of demographers. For example, the economic indicator rank of France is one of the highest in Europe (1.8); 83 per cent of couples are married, and the number of marriages has increased since 1999 (INSEE, 2002). But the beliefs of the students are supported by references to their social experience (Dubet and Martucelli, 1998), and by their frequent encounters with young people who live either in single-parent families, in a second-marriage family, or whose parents are divorcing.

Students see the traditional family – two married parents with children – as a 'natural' institution, and every other form as being exotic or strange. This is the result of a successful socialisation, which specifically induces the belief that social facts are 'natural' (Théry, 2000). For teenagers, family is based first on blood ties. Their own place in the family and their status as children are founded on such blood ties, more than on alliances, which the couple only perceive as ties. This is far more important for the children of divorced parents, because it is this blood tie that legitimises the relationship with the absent parent.

The prevailing view of relations between parents and children is that nowadays the family is democratised (Fize, 1990), freer, more egalitarian, and more open to discussion. French young people also have this understanding, as can be seen in the national enquiry on teenagers initiated by the French government in 1994. But this trend should be qualified. Girls tend to leave the family home before boys. This behaviour expresses their wish to liberate themselves more quickly from the family because they feel that they are subject to more control and to more frequent requests to do house work than boys.

Work, between valorisation and disquiet

A research study into the didactics of economics and social studies in 1998 asked 604 students, from 19 different divisions taken from 10 upper secondary schools, to write simple answers to questions about 'work'. The aim was to gather information on the symbolic value of core cognition about work (Molinier, 1994). The young people were 15–17 years old; 63 per cent were girls and 37 per cent boys. The sample was sufficiently representative, large and varied enough to offer an acceptable picture of the group which we intended to investigate (Faure and Martinon, 1999).

The results were significant in showing they held traditional conceptions: 75 per cent of the students characterise work as 'manual work', requiring physical effort. A baker or a carpenter was seen as being a 'truer' worker than a shopkeeper or a professional footballer. The gradient of freedom that the students allotted to each job depended on how they perceived the work: higher for singers, journalists, lawyers than it was for factory line-workers, and rather limited for teachers and farmers. But these global results must be qualified, because the answers varied with social origins. For example, managers' children more often said that the school manager works, and factory workers' children allotted some (relative) freedom to line-workers.

For most students, the main causes of unemployment were 'new machinery' (75 per cent) and 'international competition' (66 per cent). Collective interviews were used to better understand the structure of these conceptions (Méjias, 1999). The starting point of the students' reasoning is a compressed historical tale (with few variations): the industrial revolution created employment and prevented unemployment; unemployment today is a result of the competition imposed on companies by globalisation. 'As machinery can work better and quicker than human beings, machinery takes the place of human beings'. Every student interviewed saw un-employment as a bane, striking indiscriminately at all.

But when they imagined their own future professional activity, the same young people put forward a rather different conception of work. They give priority to pleasure (87 per cent) before stability and income; two out of three wished to draw a line between pro-fessional life and personal life. It seems that while work is still an important value – or rather, a value perceived through its depriva-tion, unemployment – either its characteristics are changing from physical pain to pleasure, or its place in the hierarchy of values is becoming lower.

Social cohesion and vectors of integration

Young people were asked in different enquiries about the vectors of integration. Work was recognised as one such, but not as the most important. The most important was often the acknowledgement of the same rights as other people (63 per cent), followed by work and voting (47 per cent) (Faure and Martinon, 1999). These results are paralleled in an empirical enquiry focussed on 37 students who were 17–19 years old in 1996. The results cannot be generalised, but here too 'work' was well placed in every answer, as that which links individuals and allows their participation in society. The boom period after World War II appeared as a 'golden age', characterised by the equation 'growth + full employment = happiness'. They used expressions such as: 'it was a euphoric period', 'there were no problems', 'the thirty years I would have enjoyed living in'. It is surprising to see this golden age placed in the close past, because, since the Enlightenment, we are used to it being set in the future, the result of progress. This could revive the Kluckhohn and Strodtbeck grid interpreting relations to time (Rocher, 1970). The association of the future with progress now competes with the alter-native conception of setting progress in the past, and representing the future as threatening. Mass unemployment probably plays an important role in this, all the more so because students associate unemployment with exclusion. This pessimistic view was partly corroborated by the *Youth and History* enquiry in France: most young people imagined a very dark future for France and for Europe (exemplified by a struggle between poor and rich people, struggles between minorities, pollution, and so on) but, at the same time, they imagined a comfortable and pleasant life for themselves (Tutiaux-Guillon, Mousseau, 1998). This disparity is important: it mirrors a conception of life so strongly individualistic that the social, economical or political context does not impact on one's own life.

In another enquiry, conducted by Gérin-Grataloup in 1998 with 224 fifteen years olds, the first source of integration identified was paying of tax and respecting law. Surprisingly, other responses achieved much lower scores. The students marked also the importance of sharing values (in Tutiaux-Guillon, 2000b). In Mejias' enquiry, young people when asked about the process of integration also approved of respecting the rules and of taking part in social and economic life, including paying one's taxes. But some teenagers also mentioned the struggle for a cause, syndicates, and demonstrations. The differences in the responses to these enquiries might be because in some studies students had only to agree or disagree, while in others they were asked to react to propositions and in others to give spontaneous answers. Differences also depend on the young people's social backgrounds, with differences observed between those from underprivileged suburbs and 'downtown'. Finally, there are differences because of the scale being considered by the young respondents: at the state level, social and legal obligations can be important, but at a local level integration in society is more a matter of getting a home and a job and being accepted by neighbours and colleagues (Tutiaux-Guillon, 2000b).

'Integration in society' raises different situations with different young people. One of these is related to social cohesion and to concrete relationships. The young people interviewed always talked of social relationships only as physical and affective ones: people speak, listen, meet, or keep to their private circles (Tutiaux-Guillon, 2000a). The best thing to solve a conflict is to meet and to discuss.

This approach evidently mirrors the young people's own experience: ties beyond the level of family or neighbourhood are difficult to conceive of or to express spontaneously. When they think of integration within a distant and larger group, young people refer 'integration' to its opposite, 'exclusion' (thus not only underlining the importance of home and work, but also the acknowledgement of one's rights) and perhaps to *criminality* (thus according importance to tax and law). Implicitly, they think that the State is the main guarantor for social cohesion. The welfare State and the legal correction of inequality are very important for them (Tutiaux-Guillon, 2000b).

Social disparity/social inequality

The following results are taken from Tutiaux-Guillon (2000a). All but two students interviewed interpreted social relationship through the idea of power. They limited social structure to two groups, one having authority over the second. The richer, more educated and superior ones, were in a position to order, force, control, punish, lead, and rule. The poorer, ignorant, and inferior ones were only able to obey and suffer, or sometimes rebel. Contempt and lack of communication signify a social gap. Only 20 per cent of the students (principally the oldest) told a more complex story. For most young people, the structure of past[2] society is strictly binary: nobility/peasantry, bourgeois/workers, leaders/people etc. (see also Lautier, 1997, Windisch 1989). This opposition does not mean only disparity, but also inequality and injustice. Both domination and the longing for rebellion are indicators of dysfunction. Hierarchy and power have negative connotations. Those conceptions were expressed also in the *Youth and History* survey: for 85 per cent of the students (who were 15 years old), the Middle Ages were 'a period when nobility, Church and king dominated peasants', and for 60 per cent 'the industrial revolution was a struggle between workers and factory owners.' Teenagers surveyed by Mejias (1996) said that contemporary society is socially split into rich and poor. This interpretation is not only that of young people: a mythical

French approach to society – as divided into two groups, people and 'important people' (*le peuple et les gros*[3]) – underlay French ideology and populist discourse – and partly still does so.

Nevertheless, the society which grew out of the process of industrialisation offers a more ambiguous and more blurred picture: the whole society is thought of as progressing, modernising, and developing; the binary image of society is tempered by an image of technical and economic progress. The industrial workers are far less well known than were the peasant of the *Ancien Regime*. Is this a consequence of teaching? Or due to a lack of any socially shared conception? In France, the worker is not a 'national symbol', the proletarian myth is not a common one, and the workers' memory is not a common inheritance. Asked why, today in their country, some people are richer, the teenagers answered that it is because of their hard work (71 per cent), or their inheritance (59 per cent), of their ability to innovate and to take risks (56 per cent). Injustice, egoism and immorality represented fewer cases: 37 per cent and 27 per cent respectively (Tutiaux-Guillon, Mousseau, 1998). We see here a hesitation or a coexistence between moral principles, condemning social oppression and exploitation, and liberalism, approving and perhaps admiring the self-made man; this indecision is typical of French youth (Muxel, 1996).

Society, between ideal and reality

We have shown above that how young people perceive society depends on their moral and social values. To talk about society is to talk of equality, of justice, of freedom, of solidarity and of tolerance. A most important value is 'communication': it combines both the right to express one's opinion, and equality through the possibility 'to speak together'; it is seen as a powerful weapon against arbitrary social and political acts. Communication transports and symbolises social cohesion and individual freedom. Those conceptions reflect an ideal: the perfect society is egalitarian and brotherly (sisterly!). For young people this is another image democracy. They also reject the quest for profit and money, which quest is perceived as the origin of inequality.[4] They judge very severely any past or present society that they see as guilty of selfishness, hypocrisy, injustice or unwillingness to understand.

The conception of past societies such as the *Ancien Regime* or that of the 19th century brings together and articulates three characteristics: inequality, subjection and segregation, the whole meaning injustice. This conception is the exact opposite of the picture of the ideal group (Flament, 1989). Society is never a net of interdependencies, nor a balance between tensions: 'true' society is harmony through solidarity and respect. This is not a 'misconception', but a basis of our culture: social cohesion is supposedly founded on justice, equity and equality (Bruner, 1991). For example, not only for the young but also for many adults, remuneration for work should correspond to effort, and not to social prestige. Justice and equality are very close to each other: justice consists in giving to everybody his/her due, and in organising an egalitarian society. In this framework, present-day society seems often more satisfactory, even if disparities are not forgotten: it is marked by technical progress, equality of rights, democracy, freedom, reduced disparity, communication, and lack of segregation. Contemporary society allows upwards social mobility for the individual who works hard and displays intelligence and initiative, and is therefore closer to the ideal.

But in another context, when they are not being asked to compare past and present societies, the younger students, and sometimes those failing academically, are deeply critical: they talk of unemployment, of violence, of pollution, of 'scheming', and of lies and hate. The older students are more optimistic: solidarity and tolerance will help overcome these faults. The young people from unprivileged suburbs surveyed by Mejias (1996) took republican values as being 'utopian values', and judged the quality of social cohesion as poor. They condemned injustice, lack of solidarity, and lack of respect between people, and diagnosed a general crisis of social cohesion. Such opinions are common. But while some signs unquestionably indicate a growing fragility of some ties, other indexes show active forms of solidarity and sociability (Weinberg, 2001), even in suburbs.

All these descriptions considerably simplify past and present society. Social complexity is not rejected, or even perceived. At the same time, the conceptions of young people mirror collective conceptions and feelings, including a deep uneasiness towards present social evolution.

Confronting school teaching and young people's understanding

In the French school curriculum, the compulsory subject which aims explicitly at social understanding is history. Other subjects such as literature and foreign languages may also contribute to reflection on social issues, through the study of novels and newspapers or through narratives picturing everyday life or by discussing social problems. Geography may also give opportunities to learn about aspects of social cohesion beyond the family or neighbourhood through lessons on population or national and regional development. Civics includes elements of social relationships such as legal regulations, and in upper secondary school consists mainly of debates on social and political topics. But the effects of those subjects on young people's understanding of society have not been investigated. Furthermore, social, civic and legal education is taught very differently from one classroom and one teacher to another to allow generalisations.[5]

History is taught during the whole of secondary education, in all sections. The stress is on French history, set in a European frame, with occasional shifts to other parts of the world when their history confronts European history. The syllabus covers not only political history, but also economic, social and cultural history. In the four first years (11 to 15 years old) students are taught a general sweep of history from antiquity to contemporary times ; the years following this (upper secondary school, 15 to 18/19 years old) are devoted to a deeper study of contemporary times since the French revolution.

Economic and social studies was introduced as a subject in France in the late sixties, when the government was concerned to improve economic understanding, and to open new paths for students, because of their increasing number. Teaching this is optional, and begins in the first year of general upper secondary school (15–16): it aims to initiate students into economics and sociology through a wide survey of major social topics: employment, family, consumption, and businesses. In the following two years, economic and social studies are a compulsory subject, but only for the students following a stream called – also – 'economics and social studies'.[6] The core syllabus for 16–17 years old is the link between market cohesion, social cohesion and political cohesion in French society. In the last year (17–18), the approach is more dynamic, and social and economical evolution is brought into question, by studying growth, social change and development, at a scale that includes Europe and the world. This pluridisciplinary teaching is intended to give students a better understanding of their society to teach some rudiments of the social sciences and of their processes.

Case 1: main conceptions and teaching are consistent

Teaching history is not only concerned with factual information about the past, but also with passing on core elements of social memory and shared conceptions of past and present. The lessons use pictures, concrete details, and dramatised tales that convey not only knowledge but that also induce implicit values. Some elements of history teaching offer a simplification of society that is quite close to young people's conceptions, for example in prints depicting a poor peasant facing a rich lord, or in caricatures of the bourgeoisie. Some teaching supports a binary interpretation of social structure – for example inviting students of 13 or 14 years to classify groups in the *Ancien Regime* into rich or poor, or powerful or powerless. Such conception of the *Ancien Regime* performs important functions: it assimilates the *Ancien Regime* into the Middle Ages (thus contrasting it with modern values); it legitimates the French revolution, which is supposed to put an end to injustice.

Even those teachers who try to picture a more complex society may fall back on rough simplifications during the lessons, for example saying that local squires were 'closer to the *tiers état* than to the nobility'. This comes from an understandable desire to facilitate quick understanding – but the student will memorise the simple binary structure rather than the more intricate one.

Conceptions conveyed through such lessons are not limited to understanding the past. They induce an understanding of society that is based on wealth as the substantive criterion for explaining differences, thus ignoring symbolic capital and taking equality in rights as being social equality. This is important in accepting our liberal society. The structural division into two groups, that might be seen as a Marxist interpretation, was already being used by the clergy in the Middle Ages. As mentioned earlier, this is a component of French ideology, and probably of our western culture.

Economic and social studies teaching can also echo young people's conceptions, more because of the content that is prescribed than from the teacher's working practice. For example 'work' is mainly studied when students are 17–18 (in the 'economic and social' stream). The content emphasises the role played by work in social integration, but it also demonstrates the limits of this role in an economy characterised by massive unemployment. This sort of analysis developed in the 1980s, with the increase in 'new poverty'. Young people's ambiguous attitude towards work mirrors this contradiction.

The same can be said of 'social cohesion' which is introduced when students are 16 to 17 (also only in the 'economic and social' stream). The lessons describe and emphasise the crisis and the dysfunction of social cohesion, as a result of the weakening of such primary institutions as family, school and State at just the time that changes in the nature of work are undermining its integrative role (Castel, 1997). The syllabus and the worries of young people echo and reflect each other. This anxiety seems rather specific to the French conception of society. From the end of the 19th century, 'growing urbanisation, individualism and crisis of social cohesion were described by sociologists with much worry' (Dortier, 2001, our translation). A hundred years later, the questions are very similar: each generation thinks that the current situation is uniquely critical. This attitude expresses anguish about the future, and a conviction that one cannot reproduce previous solutions exactly.

Case 2: the students reshape and supplement what is passed on

Generally, students spontaneously compare past societies to their own (Tutiaux-Guillon, 2000a), thus asserting the radical difference between them and condemning archaism and injustice. Students also borrow from today in order to explain the past. Thus the stagnation of either the peasants or the workers' social status in the 18th and 19th centuries is ascribed to the lack of school: peasants' and workers' children cannot rise socially, because they could not get instruction. This interpretation is not taught to students in school lessons (and is not historically valid); what they will have been told, at most, is that, one had to pay to go to a 'good' school.[7] Drawing on their own trust in schooling and on individual abilities in a democratic society, the young draw these inferences of their own. On other matters, some students draw on current events to explicate their understanding of the past. For example, current collective struggles (of the students, or farmers, or the unemployed) are used to represent or to explain the past. Sometime students – particularly farmers' children – even use their family situation as a reference point,. Young people may also transfer present day values to past societies: peasants of the *Ancien Regime* are thus said to have longed for equality and democracy.

The most frequent and powerful lever of social change, for at least 50 per cent of young, is collective struggle, and for the younger students, revolution. This refers to a simple scheme: the poorest, the most exploited and oppressed, rebel against rich leaders; either they succeed (at which point it is no longer a rebellion but a revolution), or the frightened leaders at least accept significant changes. The keys to success are strength, fortitude, and numbers. Collective social change is thought of as resulting from political change. This conception even underlies history teaching. For younger students, political change creates an immediate social change; the older students show greater awareness of the difficulties and of the length of time that may be needed. For all students, the government is the main actor in society; and the law the main agent. The contemporary claim that there will be a political solution for every social problem fits with this sort of understanding. This is close to history teaching and even more so to French social and political debates since the 19th century. It echoes the central place given to the Revolution as a founding event, and to the questioning of the political regime, as a key for social progress. It is also an echo of present-day demonstrations by French citizens: when a firm or a factory fails, 'the government must do something'. We are confronted here with an adjustment of a collective French political myth to the values of young people condemning exploitation and oppression.

Yet the same students can put forward some very different explanations from those that they have learned in school: while history lessons only refer to collective changes of masses and groups, young people introduce the idea of individual potentiality. Luck, initiative and an enterprising mind will give anybody the ability to change one's social rank, without being constrained by social structures. Most of all, for more than 50 per cent of students, becoming educated – by giving effort and interest to schoolwork – is a reliable way to rise in any society, if only one *can* attend school. Success is due only to willingness, taste and lucidity. Such accounts are grounded in an individualistic view of the world, and ignore any social and economic explanations: individuals are somehow freed from all such ties. Such explanations probably express the students' implicit trust in their own potential for success.

Sometimes collective and individual explanations of change are quite separate: when students describe events, collective explanations are detailed; when they speak of people, it is rather the individual explanations. Sometimes they unite both: rural migration, for example, is a result of individual choice (a taste for modernity, a longing for a better life) *and* of collective evolution (economy).

Case 3: the students put aside what is taught in school

In a research project on teaching and understanding Europe, we interviewed students of 15 and 17 years of age, at the end of a school year which had included learning the geography of Europe and several history lessons about European events and changes. We expected that some knowledge would be taken from the lessons to support their arguments, and we asked questions about identity and solidarity in Europe. But the young people's Europe is very different from the school topic. It is characterised by social inter-actions, friendliness and travel. The students spoke of personal experiences rather than of past cultural mixing, or of institution-alised solidarity. When they tried to make their viewpoints more consistent, they drew on examples drawn from common sense, news and everyday life, but not from school knowledge, even when they were students rated highly by teachers. The best way to know Europe and European people is to travel and meet them. School knowledge is seen as less true and reliable. Therefore cultural difference or similarities are explained through references to educa-tion, to family life, to food, to music and landscapes – everything that the teenagers have discovered themselves – and not to history or development. In the same investigation young people explained the bases for their identity by evoking territory, family, language and education – but not history. What is taught in school does not seem to them to be very useful for social life.

A similar gap between school knowledge and personal experience can be seen in their accounts of 'family'. While students seem to accept knowledge passed on by the teacher, as soon as the lesson and assessment are over, the original social conceptions and expla-nations return. This resistance can be analysed in two ways. On the one hand, young people have a social and individual experience of the topic, in which affectivity plays a major role. Though the teacher may explain to them, with examples, that 'family' is a form that will differ across space and time, the students regard as 'natural' the type of familial structure in which they have grown up. The idea that one is *socially driven to marry somebody from the same social background* seems to them incompatible with their romantic ideology of love and luck as the origins of dating and of marriage, or with their own experience of love as teenagers. On the other hand 'Family' is taught as a school topic at the beginning of the year in which students are first introduced to economic and social studies, and they probably lack the intellectual tools necessary to assimilate these ideas, that are still more difficult because the content is distant from their 'real' life experience.

For understanding 'unemployment', the question is rather different. Economics has constructed conventional categories of unemployment that are distant from common sense. To speak of someone without work as an 'active person' is not self-evidently logical. So while students accept and know the official definition of the workless (an active person temporarily deprived of their job), they will at the first opportunity reintroduce their conception of 'workless as inactive' for example, when asked to explain statistics about inactive people's low consumption (actually due to retired people's lower income). Young people, progressively integrated into society through their studies, will not accept that their efforts might not be rewarded. 'It would be ironical and dramatic in view of the studying they have completed' said one student interviewed.

Evidently, going to school is not about learning what is taught there.

Conclusion

Care must be taken when referring to 'young people' or 'French students' as if they were an entity. Social and cultural origins and contexts can give rise to very different attitudes. The *Youth and History* study suggested that specific attitudes towards history are correlated with an interest in politics and in religion, and with age and gender. Personal experience and references play a major role, not only in building meaning from one's own references, but also in questioning the world and the past, and in learning from what is taught. We need more cross-cultural surveys and research: socio-logical approaches to political understanding hardly refer to school variables (Percheron, 1993, Muxel, 1996), and teaching approaches often ignore students' social and cultural backgrounds.

But some common attitudes and conceptions are now well identi-fied. Up to this point we have referred to 'conceptions', while what we are dealing with are 'social representations', to use the expres-sion used by Durkheim, Moscovici and Jodelet. According to Durkheim, social representations are collective, shared by members of the same community: for the group they are a means to think of the world, and to think of oneself confronted with the world. They are not unique to the individual, but they influence individuals, because they provide frameworks for understanding reality and for acting in and on it. The social psychologist Denise Jodelet (1989), after Serge Moscovici (1976), defines social representations as socially constructed and shared forms of knowledge, that tend to practical goals, and that are used in the processes by which a social group constructs some common reality. They fit with people's practical experience, and thus depend on people's social place and concerns for reality. We have presented young people's conceptions as their shared representations of elements of social reality (family, job, social relationships, life etc.), that are largely constructed by reference to their social place, as children and students, and by reference to their experience as French teenagers. Their social representations do not simply organise their intellectual knowledge: they mix and structure their knowledge, affectivity, values, opinion and attitudes. We have shown how young people's values colour their representations of social facts: love, human rights, communi-cation and blooming prevail over colder and more distant know-ledge. These social representations vary in society: they depend on groups; they can too be numerous to be applied to the same object in one group: and their occurrence depends on the context. Two examples were given of this variety: how the picture of contemporary society is different when it is drawn for itself, or when it is compared to the past; and that rich people can be represented as both unjust idle exploiters and as successful hard workers.

These social representations are both content and reasoning. As content, they are often pictured as a moving and versatile periphery, orbiting around an indestructible nucleus. These peripheral aspects can be enriched or modified, for example when students assimilate knowledge that is close or consistent with their general conception. But the nucleus can only be modified through acute experience, or through change the community of reference (so, for example, becoming workless, or becoming adult). This resistance is linked to the normative function of social representations. We have no research on the structure of each social representation presented above. But, for example, 'true' society – characterised by equality, solidarity and similarity (or tolerance to difference) – is probably one such nucleus. While clearly it may be an obstacle to understand some of the complexities, it is at the same time a powerful and positive motivation for democracy!

The pedagogical organisation of lessons is probably partly responsible for the lack of success in deeply changing social representations. The dominant teaching form, that of a dialogue directed by the teacher to pass on knowledge, is an inefficient way to attain such a goal. However good the lesson, however convincing the exercises and demonstrations, the knowledge presented will fail to disturb the prevailing representations. The only examples of teaching that is effective in weakening social representations are found in problem-solving pedagogical approaches. And these are quite scarce in France.

One further problem is (perhaps) that in history, and for most of the time in economic and social studies, the students' own social experiences are not required, and even if referred to, are often dismissed as irrelevant to the lesson. In the late 19th century, school was required to develop a common identity by passing on a common culture; this imposed a rupture with what was spoken about, believed in, told, and so on outside school – which was often taken as expressing regional idiosyncrasy and archaism. In secondary school most subjects had little to do with practical or with professional life: this tradition is still active in secondary school today. Several recent enquiries into school sociology have pointed out that it is not usual for students to feel that school know-ledge is relevant of to the so-called 'outside world'. A large pro-portion of young people, asked about what they have learnt and about where they learned it, omit school, or say that they learnt what really matters outside school – from their family, their peers, and through everyday life (Charlot, Bautier, Rochex, 1992).

We therefore need not only to reflect on what content could give teenagers a better understanding of society, but mainly – and in our opinion, urgently – to devise and implement new practices that will link social experience and abstract frameworks, values and exact factual knowledge.

Notes

1. This tool, constructed by the American statistician Stephenson, was first used to explore individual personalities, and later to construct pedagogical profiles, and to introduce a group to a specific topic that is to be worked on. Canadians call it '*tri de cartes*'. It consists in proposing different assertions to the subject and asking him/her to classify them.

2. Or present, for under-developed societies.

3. The title of a book by Birnbaum, *Le peuple et les gros, histoire d'un mythe*. Paris: Grasset, 1984, dealing with political mythology.

4. We have not investigated how they can reconcile this with approbation of the self made man. Probably the quest for profit is immoral if this profit is pursued through exploita-tion, without any risk and without one's own work.

5. The syllabus consists of general topics and concepts; schoolwork is based on individual or small groups' documentary files and on discussions. See for example Tutiaux-Guillon, on OSD (www.sowi-online.de/2002).

6. The two other possible streams are 'literature and language studies' and 'scientific studies', with no or few optional courses of economics and social studies.

7. Even this is a rough simplification, confusing primary and secondary school, free charity schools and prestigious college, etc.

9

National and ethnic prejudices and their origins

Henk Dekker

Introduction

How can we explain young peoples' national and ethnic prejudices? To answer this intriguing question we will make both a theoretical and an empirical *tour d'horizon*.

National and ethnic prejudices are important fields of study because of their possible behavioural effects. They give an indication of possible future behaviours and serve to explain previous and existing patterns of behaviour. Negative prejudices may result in, for example, avoidance of those from other groups. Such avoidance may hurt the target group but may also constrain the avoiding person's own options. For example, students with a negative prejudice towards Germans will probably not consider the option of extending their studies at a German university. Negative prejudices may also create tensions in social interaction, and result in discriminatory behaviours and support for discriminatory policies, and even in violence against possessions or people. Negative prejudices do not always result in negative behaviour, because other considerations can inhibit negative behaviours, for example particular goals and values such as the wish to do good businesses and to make money, or to follow the command to 'love your fellow-creatures as much as yourself' (citizens) or to solve border-crossing problems (elites). When these inhibitions are absent or weakened, then negative prejudices can easily lead to negative behaviour. At the mass level, individuals' national and ethnic orientations can cumulatively create a public opinion and a political culture which may influence the domestic, immigration and foreign policy preferences of the elites (Jervis, 1976; Sinnott, 1995; Powlick, 1995; Foyle, 1997). Negative orientations with respect to foreign peoples and countries may ultimately have negative influences on the relationship between the countries involved and the level of cooperation with these countries, either bilaterally or in international organisations such as the European Union, especially when these countries play a leading role – for example, Germany. Negative ethnic orientations may ultimately undermine the stability of multi-ethnic societies.

In this chapter, we focus on young people. Their national and ethnic prejudices are particularly important to study because young people can become very politically active, since they have a greater-than-average preference for protest behaviour. Research among the young can determine if there is a basis for negative and possibly violent actions against particular national and ethnic groups. Another reason is that it is easier to include young people than it is adults in programmes of educational intervention aiming at preventing or reducing negative national and ethnic orientations. If we know *when* (that is, at what age) people first develop their orientations with respect to foreign countries/peoples and ethnicities, and *how* they develop these orientations, we also will have more insight in when and how to weaken – or better, to prevent – the development of these orientations in future generations

Prejudices

Prejudices can be defined as propensities to respond in a consistently favourable or unfavourable manner with respect to a given object, not in response to the qualities of that object itself, but in reaction to the category or group to which the object belongs (see Brown, 1995; Sniderman *et al.*, 1993, 4–6). A national or ethnic prejudice is thus a propensity to respond to a person in reaction not to his or her personal qualities but to his or her nationality or ethnicity, for example, in rejecting someone's application.

Prejudices as behavioural propensities are distinguished from behavioural intentions. While propensities primarily have an affective background, intentions are rationally based on beliefs about the effects of performing the behaviour (Ajzen and Fishbein, 1980).

Prejudices are not easy to measure. Often the researcher presents a set of statements to the persons being studied and asks them to react to these statements. The extent of agreement or disagreement is a measure of prejudice. For example, the Bogardus 'social distance scale' asks the respondents to react to seven assertions about a typical member of the group being studied: would admit to close kinship by marriage; would admit to my club as personal friends; would admit to my street as neighbours; would admit to employment in my occupation in my country; would admit to citizenship in my country; would admit as visitors only to my country; and would exclude from country.

The various scales used in the authoritarian personality study, including the well-known F (Fascism) scale, also depend on self-reports from the respondents (Adorno *et al.*, 1950). Such self-reports may, however, suffer from tendencies to conceal and from a veneer of self-representation, and a reluctance of people to present an unflattering image of themselves. To avoid this one also takes descriptions of the subject by observers, such as one or more peers who know them well: they might be asked to rate the subject against adjectives on a five-step scale, from 'very uncharacteristic' to 'very characteristic' (Gough and Bradley 1993). However, it is still possible that the observers are misled by the subject and do not penetrate their facade.

Prejudices as behavioural propensities are important determinants of behaviour. It is important to distinguish clearly between propensities and behaviours, because they differ in character and have different determinants. Behaviours are overt and observable acts, for example, discrimination and the use of violence. Orientations are hypothetical constructs, that is (unlike behaviours) they cannot be observed directly, and their presence must be inferred from observable indicators.

Prejudices must also be distinguished from other orientations such as affections, opinions, and cognitions. Affections include values (that transcends specific situations and are stable attributes of a person , such as equality), attitudes (favouring or disfavouring something, such as liking/disliking or trust/distrust), and emotions (strong feelings accompanied by physiological reactions and changes, such as fear; see Frijda, 1986, Marcus, 1991, LeDoux, 1996). Opinions or judgements have both affective and cognitive elements. Cognitions include beliefs, knowledge, and awareness. One has a belief or perception about an object if one links characteristics to that object. Beliefs include stereotypes of people and clichés of non-personal objects (for example, a nationality's hospitality, or a country's natural beauty).

In this chapter, we focus on prejudices with respect to nationalities and ethnic groups. They regard one's own nationality as an in-group, and foreign nationalities or national and ethnic minorities living within one's country as out-groups. Prejudices and their determinants with respect to out-groups are central.

Theories

What are the main theoretical explanations for prejudices? An important assumption is that national and ethnic prejudices are acquired and developed in interaction with the environment. Three developmental processes can be distinguished: processing one's own observations and experiences (direct contact), the process of linking earlier orientations each other and of deriving a new orientation from this unique combination (inference), and processing messages from others and accepting these (socialisation) (see Hewstone, 1986; Hagendoorn, 1992; Hagendoorn and Linssen, 1994).

Observations and experiences through *direct contact,* particularly affective experiences, are expected to influence prejudices both directly and, through their effects on affections and cognitions, indirectly. Generally direct contacts are expected to have positive effects: less negative prejudices, more positive attitudes, emotions, opinions, stereotypes, and clichés, and greater knowledge. But the effects of direct contact with foreign countries and people, as measured in empirical studies, are not always positive. The complex effects are the result of misunderstandings and selectivity in observations, selective reception, and selective retention. Observations are filtered by orientations acquired earlier. Selective observation is more likely to confirm and strengthen these earlier acquired orientations than to weaken them (Amir and Ben-Ari, 1985; Pettigrew, 1986; Stroebe *et al.*, 1988; Dekker and Oostindie, 1990; Linssen, 1995).

Prejudices are also developed through processes of mental inference. Previously acquired orientations and previously performed behaviour are linked, and a prejudice is derived from the particular combination. Three approaches to inference can be identified, because different weights are attached to behaviour, cognitions and affections. In the cognative or behavioural approach, prejudice development is preceded and influenced by behaviour. A prejudice is developed following a particular behaviour to justify that *previously performed behaviour* (Brehm and Campbell, 1976).

In the cognitive approach, negative prejudices are explained by *low levels of knowledge and negative stereotypes and clichés* (Mackie and Hamilton, 1993). That stereotypes tend to be negative is in turn explained by common psychological tendencies, such as the tendency of humans to categorise other people in groups, which are seen as equivalent with particular standards (Tajfel, 1981). Social categorisation – categorising subjects into different groups, such as in-group and out-group, 'us' and 'them' – is a universal tendency, because it is simply impossible to accurately process the huge amounts of information that people receive from their environment. Categorisation is a cognitive tool that simplifies and systematises the social and political world. National and ethnic groups are thus distinguished on the basis of biological differences, for example skin colour, other physical features, for example clothing such as headscarves, and language, or religion. Categorisation implies the diminution of intra-group differences and the magnification of inter-group differences. Tajfel's 'minimal group' experiments showed that the very act of categorisation results in in-group favouritism and negative behaviour and orientations towards out-groups (Tajfel, 1970; Tajfel *et al.*, 1971). This even happens in the absence of dependence on or competition with the other group(s). Another tendency is for social comparison, that is, distinguishing evaluatively between people – such as 'good' versus 'bad' people, 'likeable' versus 'unlikeable' persons, and 'friends' and 'enemies'. Interpreting behaviours of out-groups in terms of the in-group's values can easily result in misunderstandings and disapproval. Categorisation (such as the English versus the Germans) in combination with evaluative distinctions such as likeable versus unlikeable people) may result in cognitive dissonance (such as a likeable German) for an individual. If the individual cannot live with such a dissonance, he or she may make the dissonance containable by considering the 'deviant' phenomenon as uncharacteristic and exceptional. In case of more than a few 'deviants' the dissonance may be reduced, through internal or external attribution. 'Negative' behaviour of 'negatively' evaluated peoples is attributed internally, while 'positive' behaviour is attributed externally (Rosenberg and Wolfsfeld, 1977; Pettigrew, 1979).

More rational is 'realistic group conflict theory' (Sherif, 1966; Sherif and Sherif, 1969, 1979; LeVine and Campbell, 1972; Jackson, 1993; Quillian, 1995). This theory is based on a rational view of mankind related to rational-choice perspectives. People are assumed to be selfish and to be trying to maximise their own rewards, in terms of jobs, promotion, housing, and other scarce resources. The basic proposition is that negative orientations towards out-groups originate in inter-group competition because of their conflicting interests, due to scarcity of resources and differing values. A realistic conflict can be the result of socio-economic conflict, while an ideological conflict results from differences in political ideologies and religions (Brown, 2000). One must distinguish factual competition from perceived competition. In explaining individuals' prejudices, the individuals' subjective perceptions of conflict count, rather than objective statistics. The *perception of conflict* and the suspicion that the out-group will threaten the position of one's own group may result in a negative prejudice. This theory does not offer explanations for individual differences in perceived group threat; and inter-group competition has shown to be not the only source – or a necessary condition – for out-group antagonism.

In the affective approach to interference, the causal relationship is with emotions, values, and attitudes (Smith, 1993). Emotions have not extensively been measured in this field, but it is plausible that when children acquire their first clichés and stereotypes they also develop distinct emotions. This might be particularly expected if the clichés or stereotypes are very positive or very negative, or if they are acquired through emotional events such as national rituals (Dijker, 1987, 1991). The stereotype of Germans that some European children have cited in some studies was that they make war (Piaget and Weil, 1951). Such a very negative stereotype can easily evoke the emotion of fear. *Negative emotions* potentially form an important variable in the explanation of prejudice because they can develop early in life and last a long time. In general, one does not easily 'forget' emotions.

Acquiring negative prejudices (and negative emotions, attitudes, clichés and stereotypes) is facilitated and furthered by basic human needs for psychological security and a secure and positive sense of identity. In Maslow's theory of a hierarchy of needs (1954), the need for psychological security is second only to physiological and bodily safety needs, and precedes all other needs for love, self-esteem, and self-actualisation. Psychological security is a *sine qua non* of personality stability and emotional well-being and a minimum condition for self-protection and social survival. Its basis is biological; the nervous system tends to reduce, or at least to keep constant, the amount of excitation present within it (Bloom, 1993).

To achieve psychological security, people actively seek to develop a secure sense of identity – the perception of their own qualities continuing through time. An important part of an individual's identity is social and political, based on membership of a particular social or political group. Each group identification offers the individual a cognitively accessible interpretation of the complex social and political reality, so that he or she knows how to relate to the environment and to resolve any internal insecurities and conflicts (Allport, 1954; Tajfel, 1981; Markus *et al.*, 1985). It is thus attractive to identify with one's own people and country because it is perhaps the largest and easiest of possible categories to belong to. Moreover, people strive not for an identity as such, but rather to a positive identity. This individual need for a positive social identity and the *striving to achieve and maintain a positive social identity* is the origin of negative orientations towards out-groups, according to Tajfel's 'social identity theory' (1978, 1982, and Tajfel and Turner, 1986). People construct their social identity through these mental processes: social identifications define the individual as similar to or different from, and as 'better' or 'worse', than members of other groups. The counterpart to this is social contra-identification, including the perception and generalisation of mainly negative valued characteristics of out-groups (Billiet *et al.*, 1996). A positive social identity is achieved by social categorisation and social comparison (see above). In order to develop, maintain, and prevent an imminent loss of positive social identity, people make and enhance favourable social comparisons between the in-group and any relevant out-group. In case of freedom of choice, one tends to choose those groups which deliver the most positive social identification (such as those with high status, prestige and a good reputation). Where choice is not possible, as in the case of nationality and ethnicity, people tend to perceive mainly positively evaluated characteristics among members of the in-group and mainly negatively evaluated characteristics among members of the out-group, and to evaluate the in-group on some comparative value dimension higher than out-groups. Once developed, people will try to protect, enhance, bolster, and defend this sense of positive identity

(Hirschberg, 1993). If it becomes weaker, they try to strengthen the sense of identity. Individuals with higher levels of identity need are more motivated than others to develop positive orientations toward their own people or country, and negative prejudices and attitudes toward foreign peoples, countries and ethnic minorities (Bloom, 1993). This theory does not answer all questions. If all people strive for a positive identity and therefore make inter-group comparisons, it cannot explain differences in national and ethnic negativism between members of the same national group or dominant ethnic group and/or between countries.

The third process of prejudice development is processing information from relevant others. Socialisation theory suggests national and ethnic orientations are primarily the effect of *emotional and informative influences from relevant others* (Dekker, 1991; Farnen, 1994; Farnen *et al.*, 1996; Niemi and Hepburn, 1995). Children receive emotional and informative messages about foreign people and ethnic minorities in conversations in the family and through watching television. Later, school, church, other mass media, peers, people at the workplace, business and volunteer organisations also all become sources of emotions and information. Political elites influence the individual's socialisation directly and, via the other socialisers, indirectly. In general, people receive positive emotions and information relating to their own people or country first. In all political systems, there is an intended attempt to transfer positive national in-group orientations from the elites to the mass. This influence is well received by most of the citizens because it fulfils the important need for a positive identity. National socialisation, starting at an early age, often identifies particular foreign peoples or countries and ethnic minorities to act as contrasts. Information from extreme right-wing political leaders about foreign peoples and countries and ethnic minorities is often negative. Empirical studies from the 1960s and 1970s confirm that children develop positive clichés and stereotypes about their own people or country at a very early age. At the same time, they develop less positive clichés and stereotypes about foreign countries and peoples. Young children know the names of neighbouring countries, and a few know particular 'facts' about these countries. Based on these rudimentary clichés and stereotypes (such as 'sun', 'big cars', or 'war'), countries and peoples are labelled 'good' or 'bad', 'friendly' or 'unfriendly' (Piaget and Weil, 1951; Buchanan and Cantril, 1953; Jahoda, 1962, 1963a, 1963b; Lambert and Klineberg, 1967; Tajfel *et al.*, 1970; Jaspars *et al.*, 1972; Stillwell *et al.*, 1973). Children acquire these rudimentary clichés and stereotypes between the ages of four and eight. At this early age, clichés and stereotypes do not result from their own observations and experiences through direct contact, or from inference processes, but from socialisation. Measuring the influence of socialisation is, however, difficult: one has to demonstrate that the subject has developed a particular orientation that he or she would otherwise probably not have had. Such potential influence is traced through, among other items, correlations between the orientation under investigation and the frequency of contacts with socialisers who have the same orienta- tion. One also asks the respondents to provide their own socialisa- tion biography.

These various approaches, theories and their key variables in the explanation of prejudice can be considered as complementing each other. For example, the notion of perceived conflict and threat in realistic conflict theory could be related to the notion of insecure social identity in social identity theory. If we combine the theories, we may generally expect that most people have the most positive prejudice, and reserve their most positive attitudes, for their own people and country, and that many have outspoken negative preju- dice and attitude toward one or more foreign peoples, countries or ethnic minorities. We also may hypothesise that the main determi- nants of a negative prejudice towards a particular group are:

- negative experiences through direct contact with this group;

- negative previously performed behaviour towards this group;

- a low level of knowledge about this group;

- negative stereotypes and clichés about this group;

- negative emotions with respect to this group;

- negative attitudes towards this group;

- the perception of conflict of economic and ideological interest between one's own group and the other group;

- the striving to a positive social identity; and

- having received negative emotional and informative messages about the group from relevant others, including parents, mass media and (charismatic) political leaders.

National and ethnic prejudices and their origins

What is known from empirical studies about young people's prejudices with respect to *foreign peoples and countries* and their determinants?

The very few empirical studies of orientations towards foreign peoples and countries focus on attitudes (which are important predictors of prejudices). Two types of attitudes towards foreign nationalities are studied: specific attitudes and general attitudes.

A specific attitude is trust/distrust. Trust is part of 'good' European Union citizenship (Council of Ministers 1985; see also Dekker 1993, 1994a, 1994b). Distrust between European peoples is expected to burden European interpersonal contact and hinder further European cooperation and integration (Niedermayer, 1995). Data from the Eurobarometer public opinion surveys, conducted on behalf of the European Commission each Spring and Autumn since 1973 and covering the populations of all EU member states aged 15 years and over, showed an increase in trust among the European Union national groups till 1990 (Inglehart, 1991; Hofrichter, 1993). However, since 1990 the data show a decrease in trust in many cases (Dekker, 1999b). Mean trust among all EU citizens in 1996 was lower than in 1993 with respect to 10 out of 12 nationalities, including the large French and British nationalities (European

Commission, 1996). In 1996 only two nationalities have trust in all other EU member peoples (Irish and Swedes). Two other nationalities show little trust in all other EU member peoples (Greek and Portuguese). Of crucial importance is the low level of mutual trust among the largest nationalities. When trust is found in other nationalities, in general it is not impressive. Finally, there also was national favouritism: the Dutch have most trust in the Dutch; the Germans have most trust in the Germans, and so on. The question has not been asked in the polls since 1996. A separate study of the 1993 data showed that Dutch youth have relative low trust in Germans (Dekker, 1997). Trust appeared also to be correlated to educational level and to socio-economic status. Inglehart's 1991 multivariate analysis included only macro-level variables; he found that levels of economic development, having the same language group, having similar political systems and being on the same side in World War II explained the great bulk of variation in trust.

The general attitude towards foreign peoples and countries among young people was studied in the Netherlands in 1993, 1995, and 1997 (Dekker *et al.* 1995, 1997, 1998, 1999a) and in the Netherlands and Belgium in 1999 (Aspeslagh *et al.*, 2000). The research population consisted of 14 to 19 year-old Dutch pupils, who were attending middle and higher general education and pre-university secondary school on a full time basis. The quota samples were respectively 928, 1,076, 1,211 and 931 respondents. Each completed a questionnaire of more than sixty items. Three questions measured the attitude. One asked for the specific feeling of sympathy: respondents could rate each European Union country between 0 (very unsympathetic) and 100 points (very sympathetic). The two other questions asked for preferences, which were assumed to be expressions of attitude: ranking which European Union country they would prefer to live in if they had to move to another country; and ranking which European Union nationalities they would prefer as new neighbours from abroad. After recoding, these three scores (sympathy, country preference, nationality preference) were added together to form a score for attitude toward each country. England was one of the most favourable countries in all four years. None of the European Union countries or peoples received a negative attitude from a clear majority of the respondents. Ireland received a relative high percentages of negative attitudes from the younger two years. Germany received the highest percentages of negative attitudes in all four years. Path analyses with structural equations showed that emotions had the greatest effect on attitudes towards Germany, followed by stereotypes of the people and clichés of the country, and, in third position, direct contact. The level of factual knowledge about Germany and the attitude towards one's own country had a very weak effect on this attitude. In the 1995 study additional questions were asked about the socialisation of emotions and clichés and stereotypes about Germans. In the respondents' perceptions, the most negative expressions about Germans came from grandparents and, surprisingly, friends.

Germans and Germany were also not very popular in studies of Flemish and Walloon young people (Aspeslagh *et al.*, 2001), British young people (Cullingford, 1995; Gestettner 1996; Sammon, 1996), and young people in many other countries (Gesellschaft, 1993).

What is known from empirical studies about youth's prejudices and attitudes with respect to foreign *national and ethnic minorities* living within the respondents' country?

A survey by the European Commission (2001) in the fifteen European Union member states of 9,760 young people showed that in 2001, as in 1997, about three out of ten young Europeans aged 15 to 24 consider that there are too many foreigners in their country (29 per cent). An equivalent number thinks that there are a lot, but not too many (27 per cent). Very few think that there should be more (7 per cent). Less than three in ten believe that foreigners living in their country should have the same rights as citizens (27 per cent). Almost one in ten thinks that all foreigners should be sent back to their country of origin (9 per cent). In general, young people in the Nordic countries, the Netherlands, Luxembourg and Spain have less negative attitudes towards foreigners. The opposite seems

Table 1: Attitudes towards European Union countries and peoples among Dutch young people in 1993, 1995, 1997, and 1999 (in percentages; *n* respectively 928, 1,076, 1,211 and 931).

Country:	Positive attitude				Positive/Negative				Negative attitude			
	93	*95*	*97*	*99*	*93*	*95*	*97*	*99*	*93*	*95*	*97*	*99*
Austria	–	34	35	51	–	49	50	40	–	17	15	09
Belgium	**60**	54	49	52	31	35	34	32	09	11	17	16
Denmark	38	45	34	47	47	43	49	44	15	11	17	10
England	52	**62**	**65**	**75**	39	31	29	20	09	07	07	05
Finland	–	29	20	39	–	53	49	49	–	18	30	12
France	56	55	44	52	32	31	32	31	12	14	24	18
Germany	15	26	30	27	34	35	32	33	**51**	**39**	**38**	**41**
Greece	29	35	38	66	48	43	45	29	23	22	17	06
Ireland	13	19	25	41	31	43	43	45	**49**	**38**	32	14
Italy	37	35	41	63	46	40	44	29	25	25	16	09
Luxembourg	35	27	36	48	52	53	49	41	14	20	16	12
Portugal	24	21	28	55	50	54	52	39	27	25	21	06
Spain	34	41	46	72	48	41	41	23	18	17	13	05
Sweden	–	52	36	53	–	37	45	38	–	11	18	09

to be true in Greece. Attitude also correlated positively with level of education and frequency of travelling, a form of direct contact.

The IEA Civic Education Study of 1999, which included 90,000 students of about 14 years of age from 28 countries, measured positive attitudes towards immigrants. The scale was composed of the answers to five questions: affirmation of the rights of immigrants to keep their language, receive the same education, vote, keep their customs and generally have the same rights as other members of the country. Large majorities agreed with all five items. In 23 out of the 28 countries, females had more positive attitudes than males (Torney-Purta *et al.*, 2001).

Previous studies in individual countries have also showed that between a quarter and a third of young people have negative prejudices and attitudes towards ethnic minorities. For example, research in the Netherlands showed that more than a quarter of a sample of

1,200 secondary school pupils had a negative attitude towards foreign nationals and ethnic minorities living in their country (27 per cent). These youngsters agreed with statements such as 'Foreigners are a threat to Dutch culture' and 'Jobless Turks should be sent back to their country' (Hagendoorn and Janssen, 1983). The percentages of negative prejudices and attitudes were higher among males than females, and in pupils of lower-level than students of higher-level secondary education (Raaijmakers *et al.* 1986).

Not all migrant groups evoke equally negative prejudices and feelings; there is an ethnic hierarchy. In the Netherlands, migrants from Northern European countries and Jews evoked the least negative reactions, migrants from Southern Europe evoked more negative reactions, and Surinamese, Moluccans, Moroccans and Turks evoked the most negative reactions (Hagendoorn and Hraba, 1989; Hagendoorn, 1993, 1995). In Hungary, the majority of young people aged 18 to 19 in all three secondary school types (n = 2,600 final-year students in more than 100 secondary schools) said that they would not accept a Gypsy sitting next to them in class (60 per cent). Different minorities would reject various other ethnic groups as a potential classmate sitting next to them: about four out of ten would not accept a Romanian classmate, while about a quarter would not accept a Russian, Slovak or Jewish classmate (Örkény and Szabó, 2001). Another survey of Hungarian youth and their parents showed that young people have less favourable feelings towards certain national and ethnic minorities than do their parents (Enyedi *et al.*, 2001).

One explanation for the different prejudices and attitudes towards the various ethnic minorities is the difference in perceptions and especially in stereotypes of these groups. Studies show striking differences in the stereotypes of minority groups. For example, in the Netherlands, the Surinamese were perceived as slackers more than any group, trying to avoid all work, or heavy work in particular, while Moroccans were seen as the most selfish and complaining of all the groups, as well as intrusive and violent (Hagendoorn, 2001). Stereotypes of minorities vary according to particular dimensions. For example, mutual national and ethnic stereotypes in Eastern Europe vary across a number of countries on two dimensions. The first dimension refers to competence (e.g., the stereotypes of efficient and competent) and incompetence (slow and clumsy). The second dimension refers to morality attributions (such as honesty and tolerance) and immorality (rudeness and aggression). Combinations result in a fourfold typology of stereotype profiles: sinful-looser, sinful-winner, virtuous-winner, and virtuous-looser stereotypes. While competence attributions are strongly related to perceived economic power, morality attributions are more strongly related to perceptions of size, conflicts of interests, nationalism, as well as of perceived economic power (Phalet and Poppe, 1997; Poppe, 1999).

Other explanatory variables were included in the analysis of data from the International Social Survey Programme survey of the ethnic majority group, aged 18 and over, in 22 countries in 1995 on ethnic exclusionism, including the exclusion of immigrants and of political refugees. Educational level had the strongest relative effect on ethnic exclusionism when controlled for all other individual socio-demographic variables. Multi-level analyses, in which all contextual variables were included, showed that the poorer the economic conditions, the more the majority national or ethnic respondents were inclined to exclude immigrants. A deterioration in national economic conditions was also accompanied by stronger desire to exclude immigrants. The less extensive the social security system, the stronger the wish to exclude immigrants and political refugees; the higher the degree of ethnic heterogeneity, the stronger the exclusion of refugees (see Nowicka, Chapter 3, on the case of Poland); and the higher the inflow of asylum seekers, the stronger the desire to exclude immigrants. A significant interaction effect was that the stronger the decline in economic conditions, the stronger the effect the number of asylum applications had on the wish to exclude refugees. Two significant curvilinear effects were observed: the relative number of asylum seekers was curvilinear related to excluding refugees, and a change in the relative number of asylum seekers was curvilinear related to the exclusionism of immigrants. These relationships only held for strong and prominently visible inflows, or for changes in the inflows of asylum seekers. However, the strongest effect on ethnic exclusionism compared to all other variables, was the perception of ethnic immigrants as a threat (Coenders 2001).

Summary and perspectives

How can we explain national and ethnic prejudices among young people in Europe? Three prejudice developmental processes have been identified: direct contact, the processes of inference, and socialisation. The important inference theories include cognitive modelling, including social categorisation, social comparison and internal/external attribution processes, realistic group conflict theory, and affective models, including emotional model and social identity theory. Theoretically, the main determinants of a negative national or ethnic prejudice are: negative experiences through direct contact with this group; negative previously performed behaviour towards this group; a low level of knowledge, negative stereotypes and clichés, negative attitudes, and negative emotions with respect to this group; the perception of conflict of economic and ideological interest between one's own group and the other group; the striving towards a positive social identity; and having received negative emotional and informative messages about the group from relevant others, including parents, mass media and political leaders. Analysis of data from one of the very few empirical studies into national attitudes showed that the level of factual knowledge about Germany and the attitude towards one's own country had hardly any effect on attitudes towards Germany. The greatest effect on attitudes towards Germany was emotions, followed by clichés of the country and stereotypes of the people and, in third position direct contact. Important explanations for negative ethnic prejudices also were of an emotional kind: the perception of threat together with negative stereotypes.

The theories and empirical studies presented here suggest the following ideas about the ways that formal school education might prevent and weaken negative national and ethnic prejudices. First, the topic deserves more attention in the formal school curriculum of both primary and secondary schools – more than is now being achieved, as described in Torney-Purta et al., 1999. International exchange programmes or other ways of bringing students into direct contact with foreign peoples and countries and with ethnic minorities may be a risky undertaking: several studies suggested negative effects. When the original orientations are positive, such contact may lead to less positive orientations, because one can hardly exclude the possibility of negative experiences in another country. When the original orientations are less well defined, differentiation is possible, resulting in both more outspoken positive and stronger negative orientations. When the original orientations are negative, observations and experiences will most probably strengthen these (Wilterdink 1992). Exchange programmes have to meet many and almost unrealistic requirements (Allport, 1954, Hewstone and Brown, 1986, Pettigrew, 1986, Linssen et al., 1996) if they are to achieve the goal of reducing prejudice. One of the goals of the school curriculum should be to develop more high-level knowledge (rather than simple factual knowledge) of the political, economic and social systems of various European countries, to give insight into the living and working conditions and cultures of ethnic minorities, and to develop insight into migration structures and processes. Factual knowledge should be offered to (or collected by) students to correct unsound information and to contradict negative stereotypes and clichés. If possible, new positive beliefs should be added, that will change the proportion of negative and positive beliefs. If possible, available positive meta-stereotypes should be presented to the students: that is, positive beliefs about the out-groups' beliefs about the students' in-group. There are indications that prejudices and attitudes towards an out-group become less negative and more positive if the in-group begins to belief that this out-group has positive beliefs about the in-group (Vorauer et al., 2000). Finally, we could share our insight in the political- and social-psychological origins of national and ethnic prejudices with our students.

10

Gender(ed) issues in Citizenship Education

Florbela Trigos-Santos

What is *the problem about gender?* (Acker, 1994, p. 90)

Introduction

Is gender and education – a most controversial and problematic area in education – the discussion of the gendered educational performance of boys and girls in contemporary schooling? Or are the arguments in this debate – too often explored dualistically and antithetically as boys and girls' school achievement – insufficient for the understanding of such a complex picture, made even more complicated by the questions raised in recent post-structural research? For some reason many educationalists assume it is a dated discussion; there are many voices that claim a gender-free education. It is certainly a marginalised field of studies, though with multiple and complex frames that allow various readings, both by and for theorists and practitioners. Its implications involve identity and self, diversity and equality, distinctiveness and co-existence, private and public but also the traditional, the aesthetic, power and subjectivity, just to mention a few of the diverse perspectives and approaches from which gender and schooling have been scrutinised.

Writing this chapter offers an opportunity for reflective thought on the nature and representation of this area, on the position I hold in relation to various theories and perspectives, on my own knowledge and theoretical understanding in and of these issues. Interrogating my own interests and research in this area, I came across a major obstacle (somehow I needed to justify the irony that the invitation to contribute this chapter was directed to a member of a country where gender studies are underrepresented): what should be emphasised? What should be looked for? Too many contradictions remain unresolved, both in the literature and in the real world. I have therefore elected to adopt an eclectic perspective in this chapter, relying on my readings of some authors that have influenced the way that I look at the issues involved and, whenever possible, using illustrative examples from my own context of reference. I do not intend to contribute to a clarification of the complexity of the factors involved: this would be impossible. I will rather try to incorporate a few reminders of the place of gender as an organising principle in the sociology of education.

Historically, the analysis of gender has always stressed the difference, the split categories apparent in the male/female dichotomy: active/passive: emotional/ rational identities and their reflection in the educational context. Also, both historically and presently, gender is minimised by, among others, policy makers and practitioners who 'tend to gloss over' (Arnot, 1994) what happens in school and in society, thus reinforcing a fallacious ideology of school neutrality that remains to be challenged.

A second argument, also bearing some weight, advocates a gender-free schooling. This is thought necessary to eradicate gender bias from schooling. Both the argument and defenders assume that gender is as an irrelevant variable in education. Houston (1994) defies these arguments in proposing, rather than a gender-free of bias approach, a gender-sensitive perspective defined as 'a methodology that is self-correcting' (p. 131) and which looks for a real 'equalisation of educational opportunities'.

Just published is the first issue of *Research in Education* (my translation), the Journal of the Portuguese Society of Sciences of Education, in which Araujo (2002) was invited to write about the state-of-the-art of this field of study in Portugal, in which she assumes this to be the first time that such area is recognised, if not accepted, as integral to the field of education. For her, this invitation represented a recognition of the status conferred by the introduction in only 1995 of the first formal Masters in Women' Studies to be instituted in a Portuguese university. Even today, only a few other graduate courses offer an approach on gender and education.

Molloy (1999) expressed a similar satisfaction when invited to include a chapter on women's studies in a series edited by Michael Peters on the emergence of 'cultural studies' as a disciplinary field in Higher Education. Supposedly, gender studies, even in contexts where it is long established – as is the case of the major English speaking countries – still needs to be affirmed and its interdisciplinary authority reinforced, in order to emerge from its marginalised status. Still following Molloy, the focus of gender studies is said to be in ontological and epistemological subjectivity, and should not 'be limited to deconstructive readings of the polemics, for they are limited and repetitive but . . . requires breadth of knowledge . . . concrete knowledge and theoretical depth and range' (p. 152).

From my own and these two other expressions of surprise and satisfaction at a request for a contribution to locate gender in current publications, it appears that the attention the subject deserves is far from being over. Boler (1999) defines gender studies as 'a tentative theorising of subjectivities and emotions as a central feature, frequently overlooked and ignored' (p. 157). This theoretical contribution is in line with Damasio (1999) and others who stress the crucial role of emotions as central to knowledge construction and cognition, an important aspect in the development of identity and citizenship.

Leaving these introductory considerations as a background for disclosing where I stand in relation to gender and education, I will now summarise what is intended by the gendered nature of citizenship and education. Clarifying the concepts at stake, we must reaffirm the different meaning of sex, which is biologically based, from gender, which is socially constructed, arbitrarily and historically, by institutions and agents and based upon a concept of gender difference. Consolidated in the 19th century, largely through schooling, the female and male categories were based on an ideology of what was considered natural differences, legitimising two separated worlds, and consolidating different citizenship statuses according to their main affiliation, to work or to the family. Thus, though not living separately from each other, men and women legitimised these categories, and the public world of production became masculine while the private sphere remained feminine.

Most critical literature develops the implications of these split worlds, in the different experiences of girls' and boys' education, in particular, through schooling. All controversial issues can be derived from this structural division into male and female domains, which affects each individual's personal and social life and interferes profoundly with the quality of citizenship that is allocated to each of us. Feminist theories of gender and citizenship address this problem from a perspective of power. For them, the historical association of women to the private sphere has deprived them from enjoying full citizenship status. The values of caring, family responsibilities, staying at home and bearing children are 'invisible' qualities and activities, outside of the realm of a 'patriarchal citizenship', thus depriving women from 'the means to be recognised as worthy citizens' (Pateman, 1989, 2000 p. 248). This writer draws attention to related problems that are present in actual democratic societies, such as the 'feminisation of poverty', the 'welfare of women and children and the welfare state'. Martin (1994) corroborates that, in spite of the 'recent revolution in gender roles' and the move towards an inclusive curriculum in schools, the work-care dialectic is still prevalent in many aspects of education. Foster (1997) adds that the curriculum is experienced differently by boys and girls in schools, providing them with different preparation for active citizenship. This inequality in curriculum participation is illustrated in her analysis of the 1994 Australian Report on Citizenship Education, in which, from the thirty-five recommendations, only one dealt with the inclusion of women as 'a group with special needs' and the competences aimed to be developed were 'intended to apply generically to emerging patterns of work and the demands of adult life' (p. 59), leaving any alternative ways, such as private activities and values, out of the public sphere.

Nevertheless, it is evident from recent literature that a counter phenomenon is emerging in schools, which is challenging the assumptions of a male-dominated appropriation of the curriculum. Apparently girls are reported as achieving higher than boys, on average, in most Western societies. Yet, while some are echoing a *What about the boys!* claim for more research into 'boys' learning problems', which seems to be a reversed course of action in schooling, others stress that girls' problems and their participation as citizens are far from being resolved. Thus, I assume, the time is ripe for a full-scale reinvestigation of gender and citizenship education.

Theoretical frameworks and research in equal education opportunity

Araujo (2002) comments on the 'sporadic character' of gender studies in the Portuguese academia. However, she was able to distinguish eight categories as problematic issues in the studies developed by Portuguese researchers – these being mainly in the Portuguese educational context, but with also a few in the European dimension. These were:

(1) a social-historic perspective on the education of girls;

(2) equal opportunity politics;

(3) gender reproduction and school culture;

(4) feminism and education;

(5) youth cultures, education and gender;

(6) the development of teachers' and educators' identity;

(7) the development of professional identities due to the educational system; and finally

(8) a group of studies on gender and citizenship mainly reported in a European project 'Promoting Equality awareness: Women as citizens', coordinated by Madeleine Arnot.

The results of these studies are, not surprisingly, similar to other international published research findings that indicate the partial character of citizenship for women and the different discourses on these issues.

Citizenship education in formal schooling is supposed to attempt equality in education, and in the last two decades significant progress has already been acknowledged in statistical data. From the minimal original objective of having access to education, which, once attained, was followed by the long path from sex-segregated classrooms and schools to current coeducation, girls have gained opportunities and increased their participation in the socialising process of schooling. Equal educational opportunity is still very much on the political agenda and remains a principle of democratic education. Nevertheless, international reports (for example, UNESCO, 1995) reveal world-wide discrimination against women who are barred from attaining the most powerful and influential positions. This brings the issue of equal opportunity back to the context of schools and to citizenship education, and shows that, as well as educational policies at international and local levels that promote measures to assure equality, the social outcomes of these policies do not correspond to their professed intentions. Attempts at definition include other complex concepts, such as inclusion, justice and fairness. It has long been accepted that the problem does not lie at the individual or the group level but in the way institutions, such as school and society in general, reproduce the status quo.

A Greek study (Tsouroufli, 2002) focusing on gender and teachers' perceptions of the lived daily experience of the interactions and relationships in a secondary school, found that – as have other studies – that teachers hold different expectations according to their gender, and that those expectations were expressed, intentionally or not, in the different treatments they gave to girls and to boys. This recent research confirms again that teachers give more attention to boys, and that boys in turn receive more time for questioning and for performing, and were more often called by their first name – but were also more often reprimanded negatively for their work. This consistent pattern was also intermingled with greater tolerance and lenience shown by teachers to boys, with serious consequences for the girls, who were deprived of opportunities to express their ideas in front of the class. For the author, these findings are indicative of girls' continuing disadvantage in schooling, and challenge the assumption that in Europe (or in some European countries?) we have egalitarian schools. The need for more teacher education around these issues is evident. Arnesen (2000) stresses the importance and centrality of pedagogy and curriculum as privileged strategies for eliminating prejudice, stereotypes and institutional discrimination. Gender stereotyping is pervasive in society, and the extensive use of sexist language is permissive and reinforces beliefs in 'natural differences' that are restrictive of the full development of girl's expectations. Of particular interest here is the hidden curriculum and its associated mechanisms, which maintain the existing structures and traditional roles associated with boys and girls.

Banks and Banks (1995) also identify the major importance of pedagogy in the achievement of an inclusive and democratic education. 'Equity pedagogy involves students in a process of knowledge construction and production' (p. 153), and this will help students become active citizens because it is transformative and attends to the complexity of school cultures and social interactions in the context of the classroom and beyond. This is certainly an area where research should affect teaching and teacher education and the need to confront teachers' beliefs and myths, such as the myth of neutrality described earlier. But there is much more of concern in attempting an education for true democratic citizenship, as Giroux (1992) noted: new spaces, new relations and identities are needed in order to include difference and 'the other'.

At this point I would like to take a closer look into the issues through an account of the work of Madeleine Arnot, a prominent sociologist and researcher of education and gender. In *Challenging Democracy: international perspectives on gender, education and citizenship* (2000, co-edited with Jo-Anne Dillabough), she set the goal of exploring the gap between equal opportunity as a principle and the reality of differential treatment in schools and society. She drew attention to the new competitive market economies and to the alternative female caring ethics, and to the corresponding construction of new definitions of citizenship in which the relevancy of gender, social class and ethnicity is privileged.

In her most recent work (2002), Arnot theorises the interactions and implications between gender, class, race and educational inequalities in 'late modernity'. With her theory of gender, she was able to criticise educational systems and their reproductive capacity, using the concept of 'gender codes' derived from Bernstein and Bourdieu. Her gender code theory is a complex instrument to analyse multiple processes of gender socialisation and attribution, as well as of gender representations in school contexts, curriculum and texts. Arnot's research into the school experiences of girls of different social class, and the conflicts that may arise from their different beliefs and aspirations about the traditional sexual division of labour and corresponding sex-role stereotypes, leads her to conclude that while gender boundaries have been weakened, gender is still developing unknown and subtle forms to be found in the micro-inequalities of schooling.

In the contemporary phase of transnational processes and globalising movements, different schools and educational systems are at very different stages, and deal with these issues very differently. Citizenship education could be an excellent stimulus in schools to accommodate these new perspectives and change. As Giddens (2000) suggests, 'Education in citizenship should above all be education of the critical spirit' (p. 25).

Gendered educational performance in contemporary schooling

This section of the chapter will present a selection of concerns expressed about the differential experience of girls and boys through schooling in general, and in some particular subject areas such as mathematics and technology. The very recent trend in girls' performance in schools to achieve higher grades than boys has contributed to challenge the myth that female students do poorly in schools. However, this gain remains partially and unsatisfactorily unexplained, in that girls' performance is associated with demeaning 'remarks that it is due to hard work and rule-following rather than brains or brilliance' (Walkerdine, 1994, p. 58).

Until recently citizenship was seen as something exercised by rational beings, that penalised women and excluded them from full citizenship. Now it is recognised that women are as able of rational thought as are men, but that women are more likely to use alternative methods of making decisions. Goleman (1996) argues that they are more likely to use emotional intelligence rather than plain logical reasoning. Since Gilligan's *In a Different Voice* (1982) it has been assumed that girls are more context-oriented and that boys favour decontextualised reasoning. These preferences are associated in school with a conscious or unconscious legitimation of gender differences that confer different status to certain subjects like Mathematics.

Though this chapter is not comparative in nature, in that it aims only to discuss a broader understanding of the sometimes contradictory issues found in citizenship practices and ideologies, I bring my own context and research in the field to the discussion. In a country like Portugal, where gender asymmetries are accentuated, it is important to analyse the process and construction of social identity through the years of schooling. Though statistics indicate that women's illiteracy has decreased, that the majority of students in university are female, and that on average their grades are higher, it does not diminish the stereotyped job choices and other asymmetries in the world of production. A study by Ferreira (2002) predictably confirms the limited expectations of girls, the stereotyped professional preferences based on socially constructed and perpetuated patterns, and so on.

Another empirical research study of gender and citizenship (Seixo and Trigo-Santos, 2001) in Portugal explored young people's values and commitments, with the aim of understanding and identifying the changing patterns of citizenship experienced by 15–16 year old boys and girls in a secondary school, located in a suburban-rural area. In this study, school was more valued by girls, who felt themselves to be well integrated, rather than by boys. Girls participated actively in sports, or other leisure activities but, surprisingly, also in decision-making political spaces like student associations and class leaders. On the other hand, boys seem to prefer public spaces outside the school grounds and the community where sports are practiced. Girls felt that equal opportunities were 'almost' accomplished but had not yet been fully met – the researchers called this a 'latent sense of inequality'. These young people showed different perceptions concerning their roles as citizens. Professional success in the future was important for both groups but particularly so for boys, while girls stressed the need for a more active social role, envisaging more autonomy for themselves. Not surprisingly, both male and female students ignored any formal citizenship education in the school: for them, citizenship happens naturally, just from the fact of living together and learning from this. Citizenship education did not have a cognitive status, allowing students only to grasp empirically the stereotypes of the human dimension of citizenship.

I have selected these excerpts of the case study for this chapter because they appear to be symptomatic of something relatively *new* that is happening, and, I think, also elsewhere. School is clearly the favoured space for girls. There are scarcely any alternative places for them, while boys prefer the outside, and the local community. In Portugal girls stay longer on average in schooling than do boys, many of whom seek paid work at various levels when they leave the educational ladder. This shows some of the contradictions in this new reality. Girls, however much better educated than before, and with higher qualifications, do not attain equivalent professional success in adulthood. Our explanations are tentative, but no more so than in international literature, and suggest that schooling, though more akin to female work does not prepare girls adequately to face the fierce competitiveness of the market in the world of production. Is this a viable hypothesis? I also argue that we can understand these new developments in terms of the emergence of new transnational identity formation and the locus of citizenship as membership in the European Union allows.

More studies are needed, in different contexts, to clarify the subjectivities that underlie these rationalisations of the new trends in citizenship. Comparing the results of this study to extensive research in Nordic countries (Arnesen, 1995) for example, it is noticeable that girls are showing an enormous effort to become more affirmative, to participate actively in and out of school and that there is a growing 'development of autonomy, self-esteem, and competence to act according to their own will' – but does this mean that they are acquiring a more substantive understanding of their own identity and citizenship? Are they themselves feeling more empowered?

On the other hand, the new popular cultures that have formed around the new technologies – computers, video and stereo – are also transforming boys' experience of the domestic spaces, as the house is now becoming a pleasant place in which to be. This new consumption of the private home is potentially a common feature for both genders, but is it able to position boys and girls closer to common understandings? Though the information revolution is very pervasive, is this development going to influence, in a significant way, male values? Are we adults, both male and female, understanding the deep changes in the cultural ontology that are taking place in our schools? Are teachers perceiving and valuing these transformations, or are they rendering them invisible? In this text an important factor has not been considered: the role of the family, and in this case family gender values are important as 'mediators of class and race patterns of education' (Arnot, 2002, p. 13) in our contemporary neo-liberal agenda, in which education is a commodity and parents' choice is the focus of reform in education.

Conclusion

Most European countries are currently implementing citizenship education as part of the curriculum in compulsory schooling. Without the results of this for evaluation and scrutiny, what we can examine is the political discourse on which such a curriculum is based. We are assisted in this by the major proliferation of educational and citizenship reforms in Europe. Kingdom (1996) is concerned with the covert gendered basis of concepts, supposedly neutral, that are to be handled by teachers and students. According to her, the new discourses on rights and duties are far removed from sentiments and affectivity, which seem to be closer to the female identity (Noddings, 1999). Does this mean that policy makers are failing to understand the different trajectories that girls and boys experience in school? The results are uncertain however, the advancement for equal opportunities does not need to 'fall into the trap of social determinism . . . pessimism and a sense of fatality and helplessness' (Arnot, 1994, p. 93), despite concerns about the prevalent sense of political apathy and indifference expressed by the younger generation.

Currently, several studies indicate that there is still a female citizenship and a male citizenship in schools and elsewhere, supposedly due to the different values and prospects they hold towards their future, and the spaces they occupy in the present. Somehow, in the fear that this might become one more stereotype, I think that female citizenship is being constructed more openly in the public spaces now available to them in post-modernity. These 'new' spaces allow for the 'old' values of care and affection but in expanded activities, preferably related with the environment, and cultural and humanitarian causes (Seixo and Trigo-Santos, 2001).

Yet, as citizenship has been based till recently as more 'in tune' with patriarchal values an alternative interpretation has to be in construction as the globalised world we live in is compelling us to reformulate ideas and ideals towards a more inclusive, multi-cultural, and transnational dimension. What are the implications for our youth? I think that contemporary citizenship is ripe to incorporate the two emergent trends assumed above to be separate and apart from each other: the so called 'domestic' and the 'public' as the new dynamics of citizenship are transforming its very nature and practices and allowing in diversity and competing understandings.

The interplay between the two trends is already an ongoing process as described above in the case study that I co-authored. Whatever the results of this complex process may be, gender will always play an important role in it and no technical resolution will be effective unless a collaborative effort by both gendered human beings is sought. The changing signals strongly indicate that new identities are being fabricated in Europe and elsewhere in the world. The influence of mass media and its images is strong but also unstable and it seems that gender identity is being rapidly affected by it. What will be the consequences for citizenship and education? Who will seize the opportunity and use it for education for citizenship? The debate continues.

11

Social class and educational opportunities

Marjanca Pergar Kuščer

Despite different developmental theories that variously underline the importance of either heredity or of environment, there is no doubt that the experiences and learning opportunities given in the early years play an important role in determining one's future life. Those children with most problems in school most often come from deprived environments. There is much evidence that shows how children from different social classes achieve differently. The higher-status child, on average, stays in school longer and does better than does the lower-status child. Social class may be influential in several different ways. In this chapter I will stress the attitude of the teacher as a factor that can make a difference. Pupils who do not behave according to middle-class norms risk being considered less good students, regardless of their ability. The feeling of success the child is given in the first years of schooling is critical for his or her self-esteem. If the child feels respected and accepted, he or she sees it as meaningful to work for better academic results and to develop better relations with his or her peers.

Social and cognitive development

We usually understand cognitive development to mean those mental processes instrumental in the acquisition of new knowledge, which assist us in becoming aware of our environment. The category includes perception, memory, language, as well as imagination and judgement – it covers all those processes we use for thinking, decision making and learning. It is dependent both on one's genetic disposition and a number of environmental factors, including education, whether this be formally acquired in school, or informally acquired in the family and from friends, and through experience of life (Stassen, 1994).

Social development, on the other hand, includes personality, learning to respond emotionally, and mastering interpersonal relations. It is difficult to draw a clear line between social and cognitive development, because cognitive development is largely determined by social interactions. Adults influence children's behaviour through interaction, and children's perceptions are shaped by their experience and through communications.

Piaget suggested, in his cognitive theory (1961), that development occurs through the interaction between innate capacities and environmental events, and progresses through a series of hierarchical stages which are invariant and universal. Development is guided by the need everyone has for equilibrium: to be in a state of mental balance. Stassen (1994, p. 51) explains that Piaget meant that 'each person needs to, and continually attempts to reconcile new experiences with present understanding in order to make sense of them'. We now know that Piaget underestimated external motivation and learning, and that academic achievements result from the complex interaction between natural ability, motivation, school environment and family support (McIlvee and Gross, 1997).

The prevailing theories of psychological development, which explained growth through internal factors, such as accommodation, assimilation, control of impulses, genetic disposition and cognitive imagination have been surpassed (Driscoll, 1994). There is now a movement to accept interaction theories of cognitive development, which focus more on the social elements of development.

This social aspect of cognitive development was developed in Vygotsky's theories, whose influence has grown in recent decades and is still important. Social communication and interaction are advanced mental operations, which involve the socio-cultural phenomenon of language. Cultural differences are passed on by parents and others who motivate, lead and direct children's development. From birth, humans are social beings, capable of interaction with others; but in early infancy not yet capable of practical or intellectual action. The skills acquired through taking part in social activities are gradually internalised by the child, developing his or her self-sufficiency and independence. Cognitive development is thus largely a matter of active internalisation of problem-solving processes, including interaction with others.

Vygotsky's views on the internalisation process are in contrast with Piaget's: he switches from the idea of the *child scientist* to the idea of *child apprentice*, who acquires cultural knowledge and skills through cooperation with those who already possess them (Rogoff, 1990). As well as knowing what the child can already do independently, the teacher needs to know their potential range of development – what he or she could do with the support, help or cooperation of a teacher or a more experienced peer. Necessarily, it is the child's experience that is the starting point from where we can help him or her to achieve. Vygotsky (1986) defines the *area of proximal development* as the distance between the level of development of independent problem solving and the level of potential development which is possible with help from an adult or experienced peer.

Bruner (1996) also agrees that efficient support of learning, involving suitable encouragement through the use of symbols or social values, can accelerate cognitive development. This supports the possibility of the school being able to positively encourage and support development.

Socio-cognitive processes and prosocial development
Prosocial development – instrumental in the child's ability to co-operate with others and solve interpersonal problems – is affected

by the same factors as cognitive development. Social class can be seen to play a role in this. Bronfenbrenner (1979) defines development as the growing ability of an individual to understand his or her environment, and to influence it. He refers to this as the *ecology of development*, and suggests the ecological environment can be seen as a set of four systems.

Figure 1: Nested in the macrosystem of culture, politics and economy are narrower systems and their interconnections

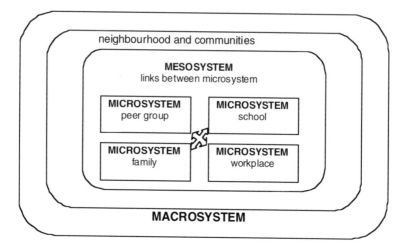

The *Microsystem* is the immediate social circles which directly affects the life of an individual. For the school child, such circles are the family, the school and the peer group; for the adult, as well as the family and friends, such circles may also include his or her workplace. Research on the influence of the family on child development is now no longer only focussing on the role of the mother, but also examines the interpersonal influences of all members of the family. The relationship between the partners affects all members of the family. Parallel studies of school and academic achievement are widening our knowledge of the range of factors that affect children's development, such as a relaxed atmosphere, cooperative learning, good interpersonal relations and peer friendship (Pergar, 1999).

The *Mesosystem* links the individual to the various microsystems. This might include, for example, a caring family environment in which parents have time for their children, and where older brothers and sisters influence them beneficially. Academic attainment can be higher, there are good friendships and contacts with peers, and there is a positive impact on prosoical development. Less satisfactory parental care in early childhood can impedes the children's ability to develop positive feelings of attachment and trust (Erikson, 1959), often reflected in unsocial behaviour towards their peers. On going to school, the ability to forge ties generally increases, but the child whose behaviour – perhaps exaggerated shyness or aggressiveness – stands out is rejected by his or her peers. Studies show that antisocial children show poor academic records (Patterson, DeBaryshe and Ramsey, 1993). Rejection by peers and academic failure in middle childhood can lead to commitment to deviant peer groups in adolescence. If this damage from lack of encouragement to social and learning in early childhood is not repaired, it can lead to problems in school and later in life (Fontana, 1994).

The *exosystem* comprises the neighbourhood and those public institutions which affect the Microsystems – including, for example, the parents' workplace. This would not bear directly on children's experience, but could do so indirectly, such as if the parents often worked long hours and subsequently could spend less time with their child.

The *Macrosystem* includes the ideology, politics, economy, values and behavioural patterns of the cultural and ethnic group – within which we can include social class. Changes in the macrosystem affect all the other systems. Thus, after the fall of the one-party system in East and Central Europe, the privatisation of companies created major changes in employment practices. Unemployment seriously disturbed family life, parents worried and were stressed about money, and the resultant loss of self-respect and other personality problems meant that sometimes children's developmental needs were neglected and they missed appropriate encouragement of their prosocial development.

The influence of social class on the identity development

Understanding of how children perceive themselves and others shows how schools might contribute to the development of identity, both national and European. Self-respect and tolerance are qualities children learn from experience of interaction with adults and other children: understanding of the self and understanding of the social world are interconnected (McIlveen and Richard, 1997). Gardner argues that interpersonal intelligence is needed to understand the behaviour, feelings and motivation of others, and intrapersonal intelligence to understand oneself and develop one's own identity (1983). In developing these intelligences – as with the other kinds of intelligence in his theory of multiple intelligences – the environment sets the level and the limits on what the individual can achieve. Theories of social stratification suggest how belonging to social groups contributes to self-image, and can determine actions towards other people and to events where people respond as members of a group rather than as individuals (Hayes, Orrell, 1993). Within every cultural and historic system three particular factors contribute to social identity: cohort, ethnic group and social class (socio-economic status). *Cohort* is persons of the same generation who share certain general social and historical influences of their time. *Ethnic groups* share such things as national origin, religion, culture and language, and minority or majority status in society: they also share moral and emotional experiences that affect their values. A comparative study of eight European countries concluded that children whose parents speak a different language at home may be less sure of their social identity (Krzywosz, Holden, Papoulia, de Freitas, Verkest, Pergar, Gocsal and Korhonen, 2002). The strongest influence on social identity appears to be the *social class* to which one belongs.

The essence of social class stratification is that position in the social hierarchy determines different levels of social reward. Though some argue that social stratification is necessary for the efficiency of society – in that certain social positions require special skills and talents, or long study and training – in reality it is often that specific skills are pivotal to status in society. In static hierarchical societies (such as those with a caste system) belonging to a specific caste prevents even the most talented from ever gaining wealth, power and prestige. In more pluralistic societies with a developed democracy, stepping up the ladder is possible but will be strongly related to the possession of material goods and academic achievements. Educational achievement, however – as will be shown below – is more dependent on socio-economic status it is on ability. Robertson goes as far as to claim that

> almost every aspect of our lives is strongly linked to our status in our social hierarchy: our scores on IQ tests, our educational achievements, the size of our families, our standards of nutrition, the chances that we will be arrested or imprisoned or divorced or committed to a mental hospital, our tastes in literature and art, our political opinions, the diseases we suffer, our life expectancy (1989, p. 167).

Nevertheless, identity is related to feelings of uniqueness, integrity and individuality. As Stassen observes: 'no one is exactly like the typical person of his or her generation, ethnic group, or socio-economic status, and each of us differs in unexpected ways from any stereotypes or generalities that may seem pertinent' (1994, p. 10).

Compulsory education and equal educational opportunities

It is compulsory for children of particular ages to attend school throughout Europe, and in many other parts of the world, but one could not argue that all people have equal opportunities for academic achievement. There is a great deal of evidence that shows social stratification is closely related to not just power, respect and wealth but also to academic achievements (Apple, 1982). Compulsory education should equip children to continue their schooling at a later stage. However, the records of individuals' school results show many differences due to social inequalities. Milharčič (2002) has grouped these in the following categories:

- inequality due to the child's background, including family, regional and ethnic background;

- inequality in the child's ability to cope with the school work, which can be due to poor adjustment to the hidden curriculum or to difficulties of a cognitive nature;

- inequality in the school environment, including teaching methods, teaching aids, status of the school;

- inequality in acquired knowledge and skills measured by tests and/or by the possibility of progressing to higher levels of education;

- inequality in life opportunities, to a large extent determined by the level of education.

This chapter focuses on the educational opportunities of children from different social backgrounds. The socio-economic status of parents influences the academic achievements of their children and their further education in many ways. This is particularly significant in economically and technologically developed societies, where knowledge is becoming highly valuable (Robertson, 1989). Marginal social groups consist not only of migrants, but also of unskilled workers and less educated young people (Rus, 1995).

Schooling is the organised and formalised transmission of knowledge, skills and values. Planning education relates to the needs of a society at its different stages of development, while educational approaches to children also depend on the prevailing understanding of their developmental needs. Although expert conceptualisations of educational needs and development are largely influenced by social, cultural and historical factors, we should not underestimate the personal experience of working with children or the life history of those expert adults who create school policies (Kojima, 1982). In the last decade a range of publications have examined educational needs for the 21 century, emphasising how educational values can contribute to peace, freedom and social justice: notable among these being *Learning: The Treasure Within* (Delors *et al.*, 1996).

School reforms and new curricula across Europe are searching for common European dimensions in education. Slovenian school reforms – at least at the declarative level – highly regard principles of *equal opportunities and non-discrimination* according to which 'the state ensures possibilities for optimal development regardless of sex, social and cultural background, religion, nationality, physical and psychological condition' (Krek, 1996, p. 39). This means that 'the transmission of knowledge in government schools should not be based on transmission of ideologically defined system of values since any such enforcement violates the child's (and the parents') right to an independent view of the world' (Kroflič, 1997, p. 271).

Against this view, conservative thinkers such as Bantock (1975) argue that egalitarianism in school is undermining of culture, and that we should encourage elite schooling for the best, and a mass education with 'satisfying' curriculum for the rest. In developing a common curriculum for all he does not see equal experience for all children, but rather an open selection in which those who should be the recipients of the common experience become its victim.

The aim of compulsory education should and must be acquisition of the basic knowledge and skills which will enable all children to approach the social and natural environment independently, efficiently and creatively and which will help them develop their awareness of belonging to a certain cultural tradition.

Socio-economic status and academic achievements of the children: some research data

There is considerable evidence that children from different social classes have different levels of educational achievement. On average, higher-status children stay in school longer and do better than do lower-status children. Social class is influential in a variety of ways. Academic achievements are increasingly significant in current times in western societies: good school results lead to further education; higher education leads to better employment opportunities; better employment means higher income. However, as Jencks (1972) points out, social inequality is *related* to academic achievements but not *caused* by them. Differences in social and economic status mean that children are differentially equipped to take advantage of opportunities, from the earliest stages of their education. State schools are not designed to engage all children intellectually and emotionally: those from wealthier families are educationally privileged, in the sense that their parents can pay for private schools where they have better conditions, which lead to higher academic achievements. However, children from similar wealthier backgrounds are also higher achievers in state schools. Many studies indicate that students of the same ability will achieve different results, and that their grades correspond to their social and economic status. In other words, a child's social-economic status is a more accurate predictor of his or her school success than any other factor, including IQ and personality traits.

The case in Slovenia

Before the social and political changes that led to independence, there was a wide, systematic and very complex study in Slovenia that looked at differences in academic achievement, intellectual ability, occupational and educational aspirations, study habits, style of learning and other personality characteristics to examine how these might relate to their socio-economic status (Toličič and Zorman, 1977). The study was intended to alert people to the existence of some very difficult conditions for some children, and to promote necessary school reforms and other changes for these children. Many independent variables were included, such as those related to the parent's standard of living, as were many dependent variables, such as school grades, test results, reading levels, IQ, the results of questionnaires on learning habits, and of a special questionnaire to determine pupils' occupational aspirations and expectations. Teachers provided records of items such as how often parents attended parent-teacher meetings, and head teachers provided records of schools and teachers. The results showed the important role of socio-economic and demographic factors in the development of the child's personality, and the great extent to which they influenced the child's success in school. They showed that children with parents with a low level of education and standard of living achieved less in school and had lower occupational and educational aspirations.

Research by Makarovič (1984) confirmed how social inequality influenced the realisation of the child's intellectual potential. His research focused on those whose achievements in school were lower than their actual abilities, and who moved into occupations less demanding of their potential. He found that children with high potential intelligence from families of low social status did not achieve academically, did not take up further education, and had lower-status occupations. On the other hand, children from higher social status families who were less academically able nevertheless did achieve better academic results, took their education beyond compulsory schooling, and generally overachieved. A more recent statistical analysis of data by Čuk and Peček (2002) on parental level of education and children's academic achievement confirmed that the parents' level of education significantly determined the child's potential to achieve academically. Even though School Legislation I (1996, p. 10) states that 'children from socially less advantaged surroundings should be given the same opportunity for education', this research shows that schools still reinforce social inequality between children.

Research results such as these do not differ from those found in other countries, where the child's socio-economic status may be measured by a wide variety of factors, including the parents' education, their income, provision of subsidised school meals, and sometimes even by 'race' or ethnicity or refugee status.

Parent's values

There is an apparent link between the parents' aspirations and expectations and their child's educational experience. If the family expects the child to continue his or her education through high school and on to university, then the child is more motivated to do so. As Robertson puts it,

> middle-class and upper-class parents are inclined to take it for granted that their children will do well academically. Lower-class parents are much less likely to make the same assumption; they may instead hope that their child will become apprenticed to a trade. (1989, p. 284)

He argues that children from higher socio-economic backgrounds, with parents who themselves have higher education, live surrounded by books and educational toys – they are exposed to values which lead to higher achievements in school, and also often live in smaller families where they get more attention: they become socialised earlier, and this maximises their learning potential.

A further important factor is cultural motivation for schooling (Kao, 1995), and this also stems from the values of the parents. There is the well known example of children from eastern Asia who score very highly in international comparisons of knowledge in mathematics and science, such as the TIMSS studies (The International Mathematics and Science Studies). Some have interpreted these results as a consequence of long and ruthless hours of drilling in results-oriented schools. However, Asian refugee families in American schools also scored better than their American peers at the same schools (Caplan, Choy and Whitmore, 1992). Researchers from Michigan University interviewed the parents of some of these children in Ann Arbor: even though the parents were poorly educated and spoke little English, they had high respect for school for their children, and put considerable effort into setting them realistic goals, priorities and standards. Children's achievement can be positively affected if the parents believe that their actions can make a difference and lead to achievement. They saw education as playing an important role in integration. These children spent more time doing homework than their American peers, and the whole family participated in this.

Stevenson (1992) suggests that motivation to learn enables children to experience satisfaction when they solve a problem, rewarding the effort they have put in. Acquiring knowledge becomes a satisfying experience, so that the 'common belief that results-oriented Asian schools are diminishing children's enjoyment is a stereotype, as most children there seem to be quite happy, despite the high standards and discipline' (1992, p. 36). Some with expertise in both Japanese and European educational systems believes that European systems may pay insufficient attention to children in the early years when they are most developing their potential (Elschenbroich, 1995). Japanese teachers expect from parents to cooperate with children: for example, every morning the mother will prepare rice for the child to take to the kindergarten for lunch, even though children have all their meals provided there. In this way the mother's attention reaches the child even when he/she is learning to socialise with his/her peers. Studying educational approaches in other cultures widens horizons and understanding when examining our own culture's educational approaches.

The teacher's role in pupil's social learning

Most empirical studies show a clear link between the social status of the child's family and his/her achievement in schools, but it is also clear that school can compensate for social deprivation, even though they do not always provide adequately for it. Children who have problems in schools most often come from deprived environments (Smith, Cowie and Blades, 1998). Their patterns of behaviour may be an obstacle to efficient communication and co-operation with others, and may cause misunderstandings and provoke rejection, which can in turn lead to failure and to various forms of antisocial behaviour. When the child behaves in a socially appropriate manner, he or she demonstrates that they recognise and understand social messages, and know how to communicate in a manner suited to the situation and its purpose (Pučko, 2002). Most children who live in a social environment that enforces rules similar to those applied in school do not experience a problem. But children who have never learned to express their feelings and views in a suitable manner have difficulties in overcoming misunderstandings and conflicts, and also in acquiring and demonstrating their knowledge.

The *White Paper on Education in the Republic of Slovenia* (Krek, 1996, p. 22) suggests that schools should organise for children from socially disadvantaged background 'extracurricular activities to make up for the socialisation deficiency and thus break the vicious circle of academic failure,' while at the same time, they should not lower standards of knowledge and assessment: instead, new mechanisms should be put in place 'to equalise the starting point providing all with equal educational opportunities'.

Governments in many countries have spent large sums reduce class sizes in primary schools: while noise and disruptive behaviour of children in the classroom have decreased, their knowledge has not increased (Ehrenberg *et al.*, 2001). While a smaller number of pupils in the classroom could help children develop better study habits, higher self-esteem and other beneficial cognitive traits, research seems to suggest that teachers are not changing their teaching methods. The key to quality education remains the teacher. Belief in the power of knowledge and the ability of their pupils to learn (Milharčič, 2002) can induce changes in the learning of the less advantaged children.

In *Under one roof – On becoming Turk in Sweden*, Narrowe (1998) explains why she is upset by explanations of the behaviour of migrants in school by cultural difference: colleagues who do this, she suggests 'seemed to essentialise immigrant-ness, to reify immigrants' cultures, and to avoid focusing on the daily production of commonalities' (Narrowe, p. 2). Teachers should not use their own stereotypes to put such children in a cultural box, because it is not the culture that solves mathematics problems, nor does the pupil's culture predetermine the amount of knowledge the geography teacher can expect from him or her.

Robertson (1989) argues that most teachers have middle-class values. These values affect their assessment of events and decisions to act (Musek, 1993) and operate as the standard by which views are measured and assessed. Children who do not behave in accordance with the teacher's standards risk being seen by the teacher as 'worse', regardless of their abilities. The experiences children gain in the first years of schooling are extremely important for their self-image. If the child feels that he or she is respected, it makes sense for him or her to work harder to learn and to have better relations with peers. Studies of teachers' personal traits and interpersonal relations among children in the lower primary school have shown that the degree to which children like to go to school, and the level of pleasure and satisfaction they experience in school, depends to a great extent on the teacher's sensitivity to the children's psychological needs for belonging and competence (Pergar, 2001). A well-prepared curriculum in not sufficient for successful teaching and learning.

Lewis (1995) looked for the reasons for high academic achievements among Japanese children: her initial hypotheses centred on their longer academic year, strictly prescribed curriculum and the considerable family support. She concluded eventually that the main reason for their success is the early positive experience children get in the first years of primary school. In the first year, the child's need for friendship, belonging and the opportunity to participate in school life are satisfied. Children are not divided into classes according to their abilities, but master the programme together, because cooperation and perseverance are recognised as important values. The classroom community is based on the feeling of belonging, which children develop with their teacher's help: there is no competition. Every child is made responsible to lead the class for a period, irrespective of his or her academic achievements. Discipline is based on understanding the importance of kindness and responsibility for the community, not on rewards and punishment.

To develop a more complex understanding of the child's educational opportunities, it is necessary to take into account not only his or her biological attributes, but also the social, cultural and economic background in which the education takes place. Children learn when they feel safe, comfortable and suitably motivated. Social interaction is more than just a teaching method – it is the source of higher mental processes. For this reason, efforts to reform education and provide equal opportunity for all children must also include training better and more creative teachers who will care for children and who understand that classroom teaching needs to develop the child's feeling of belonging and mutual understanding, as well as academic learning.

Notes on Contributors

Sigrún Adalbjarnardóttir is Professor of Education in the Faculty of Social Sciences at the University of Iceland. Her research interests are in the area of teacher professional development, citizenship education with a focus on promoting students' social and ethical growth, and adolescent risk-taking behaviour with a focus on how various educational, psychological and sociological factors relate to adolescent substance use. In each of these research areas she has conducted longitudinal studies and has published numerous journal articles and book chapters on her research. Within the Ministry of Education she has written teacher guides and textbooks in social studies for elementary school students and more recently on interpersonal issues and ethical concerns. She is the National coordinator of CiCe (Children's Identity and Citizenship in Europe) for Iceland and a member of the Group for the Study of Interpersonal Development (GSID) at Harvard University, School of Education.

Henk Dekker is Professor with a chair for the Social-Scientific Study of the Germany-Netherlands Relationships at Utrecht University and is Associate Professor of Political Science at Leiden University (both in The Netherlands). He is director of the Utrecht University European Research Centre on Migration and Ethnic Relations. He is vice-chair of the International Political Science Association's Research Committee on Political Socialization and Political Education and a member of the Netherlands Political Science Association board. His research focuses on explaining political behaviour and orientations, including voting behaviour, national identities including nationalism, and national stereotypes. His courses focus on political psychology, political socialization, and national identities and stereotypes.

Anette Emilson has lectured at the University of Kalmar (Sweden) since 1998, where she educates Early Years teachers. Previously, she graduated from Göteborg and worked as a pre-school teacher. She is also a docotral student at the Department of Education at Göteborg University. Her research interest is how democratic values are fostered with children under three within Swedish preschools and in the socialisation of young children and how they construct and develop social identities and citizenship in a preschool context.

Tiiu Kadajane is a Lecturer in the Department of General Education, University of Tartu (Estonia). Her research interests are in the area of school social work (*Handbook of school social work for head teachers, form teachers, teachers and social workers* (2001) Tartu: University of Tartu, (in Estonian)). She is also involved in research on teacher professional development at the University of Tartu.

Edgar Krull is Professor of General Pedagogy at the University of Tartu (Estonia) where he is the Head of the Department of General Education and the Estonian National Coordinator for the CiCe Thematic Network. His research interests are teacher professional development (*Estonian teachers' educational attitudes and beliefs at the turn of the millennium* (2002) Tartu: University of Tartu (in Estonian); *Evaluation of teaching* (1998) TUP (in Estonian); 'Teacher Professional Development in Estonia' in *Journal of Teacher Education in Europe*, 24, 2, (2001)) and the methodology of teaching educational psychology (*Handbook of Educational Psychology* (2000/01) TUP, in Estonian).

Marjanca Pergar Kuščer received her Ph.D in psychology from the University of Ljubljana in 1999. She is Assistant Professor of developmental psychology in the Department of Basic Education Studies at the University of Ljubljana, Faculty of Education, where she contributes to both undergraduate and postgraduate teacher training programmes. Her main areas of research are primary school teacher education, the developmental needs of children in school, cross-cultural comparison, values, the creativity of teachers and pupils, equal educational opportunities, the development of identity and conceptual development. She has participated in a variety of international and national research projects.

Jane Mejias graduated in political and social sciences, after which she taught economics and social sciences in high school. In 1999 she joined the Institut Universitaire de Formation des Maîtres of Lyon (France), where she is responsible for initial teacher training in these subjects. She is part in a research group of academics and secondary teachers investigating the didactics of economics and social sciences: her focus is on state, work and the market, and she has investigated students' conceptions of these terms. She leads another research group on teaching controversial topics. She contributes to the site *www.brises.org*, which examines the contents of economics and social sciences taught in the final year of high school. Her most recent publications are 'La relation modernisation/chômage' (The relationship between modernisation and unemployment), in *DEES*, 118 (Dec 1999) Paris: CNDP, and 'BRISES, un outil coopératif porteur de trans-formations' (BRISES, a cooperative tool for transforming teaching) in *Teaching economics, Enseigner l'économie, Actes du colloque de Clermont Ferrand* (2003) L'Harmattan.

Marzenna Nowicka is a senior lecturer at the University of Warmia and Mazury in Olsztyn (Poland), and has a Doctor of Humanities in pedagogics. She is the author of many papers published about particular aspects of children's education. Her research interests are in the area of language in school interactions, children's social learning and learning about society in the Polish educational system.

Alistair Ross is Professor of Education at the London Metropolitan University (UK), where he is the Director of the Institute of Policy Studies in Education and the International Coordinator for the CiCe (Children's Identity and Citizenship in Europe) Thematic Network. His research interests are in the area of the school curriculum (*Curriculum: Construction and Critique*, Falmer, 2000), children's social and political learning, the careers of teachers (co-editor, *The Crisis in Teacher Education*, Trentham, 2002), citizenship education, and access to higher education (co-author, *Higher Education and Social Class*, Falmer/Routledge, 2003). He is series editor for European Issues in Children's Identity and Citizenship.

Beata Krzywosz-Rynkiewicz is Doctor of Philosophy (PhD) in psychology, a graduate of Warsaw University; and presently a senior lecturer at the University of Warmia and Mazury in Olsztyn (Poland). She was co-founder and head teacher of the experimental 'Żak' primary school in Olsztyn. For thirteen years she has conducted lectures and workshops for initial teacher training students and teachers in-service education, and has written about a dozen papers published in Poland and abroad. Her research interests are in the field of children's social learning and learning about society, self-responsibility and social competence. She is a member of several international research and training programmes (such as CiCe).

Ingrid Pramling Samuelsson is a professor and coordinator for early childhood education at the Department of Education, Göteborg University (Sweden). Her background is as a preschool teacher, and she was appointed to the first chair in early childhood education in Sweden in 1996.

Her research mainly focuses on how children create meaning and make sense of different aspects of the surrounding world, in the context of pre-school (day care and kindergarten). Another research interest is teachers' professional development. Professor Pramling Samuelsson has been consulted by the Ministry of Education, the National Agency for Education, and the Department of Social Welfare and Health on questions about children. She is also president of Swedish OMEP (Organisation Mundiale pour l'Éducation Préscolaire).

Julia A. Spinthourakis and **John M. Katsillis** are both faculty members of the Department of Elementary Education of the University of Patras (Greece). She is an Assistant Professor specialising in multilingual/ multicultural education. Julia's interests and publications are in the area of second language teaching, social studies, teacher beliefs and culture in communication and the classroom. John is an Associate Professor specialising in Sociology of Education, Social Stratification, and Social Statistics and Research methods. His interests and publications are in the area of socialisation, achievement and evaluation and social statistics.

Florbela Trigo-Santos is Assistant Professor in the Department of Education in the Faculty of Sciences at the University of Lisbon (Portugal). Her research areas are in the field of intercultural education, gender, and women leadership in schools. She has published papers in these areas, and a book on teachers' cultures (IIE, 1996). Currently she is Vice-President in the Portuguese Education Administration Forum, as well as the CiCe's National coordinator for Portugal.

Nicole Tutiaux-Guillon has a doctorate in history didactics (1998). She is *maître de conférences* in the Institut Universitaire de Formation des Maîtres of Lyon (France), where she teaches didactics of history, geography and civics. She has been responsible for several research projects conducted in the INRP (Paris) from 1990 to 2000, in history and geography didactics, the most recent on teaching and learning in Europe. At the same time she had been involved in European research in the *Youth and History* project, and, since 2001, the CiCe project. Her present research focuses on the links between the aims of school history and geography, the contents really taught, and the teaching practices. Her most recent books are *L'Europe entre projet politique et objet scolaire* (INRP, 2001) and (edited with D. Nourrisson) *Identités, mémoires, conscience historique, actes du colloque des 8–11 octobre 2001* (P.U.S.E., 2002).

Hugo Verkest has been lecturer in the School of Education (Normaal-school) at the Torhout campus of the Katholieke Hogeschool Zuid-West-Vlaanderen (Belgium) since 1989 and lecturer in methodology in the Higher Episcopal Institute of Education in Brugge since 1998. He is co-author of textbooks on religion and ethics for primary and secondary school (Roeach, Respons, Tov) and was editor of the periodical *Korrelcahier* (1985–1995), which dealt with handling conflict, the influence of the media and children's identity. He is currently engaged in projects on world heritage, rural identity, refugees, sustainable development and equal opportunities in education. He is International coordinator of RENO-KATHO (for primary education), National CiCe coordinator for Belgium and for EFTRE (the European Forum for Teachers in Religious Education).

Bibliography

Acker, S. (1994) *Gendered Education: sociological reflections on women, teaching and feminism*, Buckingham: Open University Press.

Adalbjarnardóttir, S. (1993) Promoting children's social growth in the schools: An intervention study. *Journal of Applied Developmental Psychology, 14*, 461–484.

Adalbjarnardóttir, S. (1994) Understanding children and ourselves: Teachers' reflections on social development in the classroom. *Teaching and Teacher Education, 10*, 409–421.

Adalbjarnardóttir, S. (1999) Tracing the developmental processes of teachers and students: A sociomoral approach in school. *Scandinavian Journal of Educational Research, 43,* 57–79.

Adalbjarnardóttir, S. (2001) Cultivating citizenship awareness: The school setting. In Ross, A. (ed.) *Learning for a Democratic Europe* (pp. 167–173). London: CiCe.

Adalbjarnardóttir, S., and Selman, R. L. (1989) How Children Propose to Deal with the Criticism of their Teachers and Classmates: Developmental and Stylistic Variations. *Child Development, 60,* 539–551.

Adalbjarnardóttir, S., and Selman, R. L. (1997) 'I feel I received a new vision': An analysis of teachers' professional development as they work with students on interpersonal issues. *Teaching and Teacher Education, 13,* (4), 409–428.

Adorno, Th. W., E. Frenkel-Brunswik, D. J. Levinson, and R. N. Sanford (1950) *The authoritarian personality*. New York, NY: Harper and Row.

Ajzen, I., and Fishbein, M. (1980) *Understanding attitudes and predicting social behavior.* Englewood Cliffs, NJ: Prentice Hall.

Allport, G. (1954) *The nature of prejudice*. Garden City: Doubleday. Reading, MA: Addison-Wesley.

Alvestad, M., and Pramling Samuelsson, I. (1999) A Comparison between the National Preschool Curricula in Norway and Sweden, *Early Childhood Research and Practice,* 1(2). http://www.ecrp.uiuc.edu/v1n2/index.html

Amir, Y., and R. Ben-Ari (1985) International tourism, ethnic contact, and attitude change. *Journal of Social Issues*, 41,3, 105–115.

Anderson, M. (1999) Children in between: Constructing identities in the bicultural family. *The Journal of the Royal Anthropological Institute*, 5(1), 13–26.

Apple, M. W. (1982) *Education and power: Reproduction and contradiction in Education.* London: Routledge and Kegan Paul.

Araujo, H. C. (2002) 'Ha ja lugar para algum mapeamento nos estudos sobre genero e educacao em Portugal? Uma tentativa exploratoria' (Is there already place for some mapping in gender and education in Portugal? An exploratory effort). *Investigar em Educacao.* SPCE, V1, 1, pp. 101–145.

Arnesen, A. (1995) *Gender and equality as quality in school and teacher education,* Oslo: Oslo College School of Education.

Arnesen, A. (2000) 'Relacoes Sociais de Sexo, Igualdade e Pedagogia na Educacao no Contexto Europeu' (Sexual Social Relations, Equality and Pedagogy in education in the European Context), *ex aequo*, 2/3, pp. 125–140.

Arnot, M. (1994) 'Male Hegemony, Social Class, and Women's Education' in Linda Stone (ed) *The Education Feminist Reader.* New York, NY: Routledge.

Arnot, M. (2002) *Reproducing Gender? Essays on educational theory and feminist politics,* London: Routledge/ Falmer.

Arnot. M, and Dillabough, J. (2000) 'Feminist Political Frameworks: new approaches to the study of gender, citizenship and education', in M. Arnot and J. Dillabough (eds) *Challenging democracy: International Perspectives on Gender, Education and Citizenship,* London: Routledge/Falmer.

Askell-Williams, H, and Lawson, M. J. (2001) Mapping students' perceptions of interesting class lessons. *Social Psychology of Education, 5,* 127–147.

Aspeslagh, R., F. Boen, H. Dekker, H. Linssen, R. Pepermans, N. Vanbeselare, and V. Yzerbyt (2000) *België en Nederland.* (Belgium and The Netherlands). The Hague: Netherlands Institute of International Relations 'Clingendael'.

Asplund Carlsson, M. Pramling Samuelsson, I., and Kärrby, G. (2001) *Strukturella faktorer och pedagogisk kvalitet i barnomsorg och skola – En kunskapsöversikt.* (Skolverkets monografiserie.) Stockholm: Liber distribution.

Baldwin, J. (2002) *Socialisation.* http://www.soc.ucsb.edu/faculty/baldwin/classes/soc142/abnormalsczn.html

Bandura, A. (1977) *Social learning theory.* Englewood Cliffs, NJ: Prentice-Hall.

Bandura, A. (1986) *Social foundations of thought and action: A social cognitive theory.* Englewood Cliffs, NJ: Prentice-Hall.

Banks, C. A. M., and Banks, J. A. (1995) Equity Pedagogy: An Essential Component of Multicultural Education, *Theory into Practice*, 34, N 3. pp. 152–158.

Bantock, G. H. (1975) Equality and education. In B. Wilson (ed.) *Education, equality and society.* London: Allen and Unwin.

Barnombudsmannen. (2000) *Kompanjoner eller dekoratione.* http://www.bo.se

Baumrind, D. (1971) Current patterns of parental authority. *Developmental Psychology Monograph, 4* (1, Part 2).

Belton, L. (1996) What our teachers should know and be able to do: A student's view. *Educational Leadership, 54,* 66–68.

Biblioteczka Reformy no. 7 (1999) *I etap edukacyjny, kształcenie zintegrowane.* Warszawa: MEN.

Bidwell, L. D. M., and Vander Mey, B. J. (2000) *Sociology of the family: Investigating family issues.* Needham, MA: Alleyn and Bacon.

Bigelow, B. J. (1977) Children's friendship expectation: A cognitive-developmental study. *Child Development*, 48, 1. pp. 246–253.

Bigelow, B. J., and La Gaipa, J. J. (1975). Children's written descriptions of friendship: a multidimensional analysis. *Developmental Psychology*, 11, 6 pp. 857–858.

Billiet, J., R Eisinga, and P. Scheepers, (1996) Ethnocentrism in the low countries: a comparative perspective. *New Community*. 22, 401–416.

Bińczycka, J. (1997) *Między swobodą a przemocą w wychowani*. Kraków: Oficyna Wyd. Impuls.

Birch, S. H., and Ladd, G. W. (1996) Interpersonal relationships in the school environment and children's early school adjustment. The role of teachers and peers. In J. Juvonen and K. Wentzel (eds.), *Social Motivation: Understanding children's school adjustment* (pp. 199–225). Cambridge, UK: Cambridge University Press.

Blankemeyer, M., Flannery, D. J., and Aszsonyi, A. T. (2002) The role of aggression and social competence in children's perceptions of the child-teacher relationship. *Psychology in the Schools*. 39, 293–304.

Bloom, B., Englehart, M., Furst, E., Hill, W., and Krathwohl, D. (1956) *Taxonomy of educational objectives: The classification of educational goals*. Handbook 1, *Cognitive domain*. New York, NY: Longmans Green.

Bloom, W. (1993) *Personal identity, national identity and international relations*. Cambridge: Cambridge University Press.

Bloss, T. (1996) 'La "démocratisation" des relations parents-jeunes', in La famille malgré tout, *Panoramiques* 25, Paris.

Boler, M. (1999) 'Disciplined Absences: Cultural Studies and the missing discourse of a feminist politics of emotion' in Michael Peters (ed) *After the Disciplines: The emergence of Cultural Studies*. Westport, Connecticut: Bergin and Garvey.

Brehm, J. W. and D. Campbell (1976) *Ethnocentrism and intergroup attitudes*. New York, NY: Wiley.

Bronfenbrenner, U. (1979) *The ecology of human development: Experiments by nature and design*. Cambridge, MA: Harvard University Press.

Brophy, J. E., and Good, T. L. (1974) *Teacher-student relationships: Causes and consequences*. New York, NY: Holt, Rinehart and Winston.

Brown, M. D. (2000) Conceptualising racism and islamophobia. in Walter, J. and Verkuyten, M. (eds.). *Comparative perspectives on racism*. Aldershot: Ashgate. 73–90.

Brown, R. (1995) *Prejudice; its social psychology*. Cambridge, MA: Blackwell.

Bruner, J. (1991) *Car la culture donne forme à l'esprit*, Paris: ESHEL.

Bruner, J. S. (1996) *The culture of education*. Cambridge MA: Harvard University Press.

Buchanan, W., and H. Cantril (1953) *How nations see each other. A study in public opinion*. Urbana, Illinois: University of Illinois Press.

California Tomorrow (2002) How children develop a sense of identity. http//teacher.scholastic.com/professional/teachdive/identity.htm.

Caplan, N., Choy, M. H., and Whitmore, J. K. (1992) Indochinese refugee families and academic achievement. *Scientific American*, February, 36–42.

Castel, R. (1995) *Les métamorphoses de la question sociale*. Paris: Fayard.

Charlot, B., Bautier, E., and Rochex, J.-Y., (1992) *Ecole et savoir dans les banlieues et ailleurs*. Paris: Armand Colin.

Cillessen, A. H. N. (1997) Sociometric Status, Social Self-Perceptions, and the Development of School Adjustment in Middle Childhood. Paper presented at the Biennial Meeting of the Society for Research in Child Development (62nd, Washington, DC, April 3–6, 1997).

Clark, R. M. (1990) Why disadvantaged students succeed. *Public Welfare*. Spring, 17–23.

Coenders, M. (2001) Nationalistic attitudes and ethnic exclusionism in a comparative perspective. An empirical study of attitudes toward the country and ethnic immigrants in 22 countries. Dissertation. Nijmegen: Catholic University Nijmegen.

Cohen, P. A. Kulik, J. A., and Kulik, C.-L. C. (1982) Educational outcomes of tutoring: A meta-analysis of findings. *American Educational Research Journal*, 19, 2. pp. 237–248.

Cohn, D., Patterson, C., and Christopoulos, C. (1991) The family and children's peer relations. *Journal of Social and Personal Relationships*, 8, 315–346.

Coleman, J. (1988) The creation and destruction of social capital: Implications for the law. *Journal of Law, Ethics and Public Policy*, 3, 375–404.

Coleman, J. (1990) *Foundations of social theory*. Cambridge, MA: Belknap Press of Harvard University Press.

Collinson, V., Killeavy, M., and Stephenson, H. J. (1999) Exemplary teachers: Practicing an ethic of care in England, Ireland, and the United States. *Journal for a Just and Caring Education, 5*, 349–366.

Coplan, R. J., Gavinski, Molina, M-H., Galce-Seguin, D. G., and Wichmann, C. (2000) When Girls Versus Boys Play Alone: Nonsocial Play and Adjustment, *Kindergarten Developmental Psychology*, 17(4), 464–465.

Council of Ministers of the European Community (1985) *Report of the Ad Hoc Committee on a People's Europe*. Brussels: Council of Ministers.

Čuk, I., and Peček, M. (2002) Šola in pravičnost (School and justice) in Pučko V. C. R. *et al. Zaključno poročilo projekta: Identifikacija kriterijev za vrednotenje pravičnosti v izobraževanju*. Ljubljana: Pedagoška fakulteta.

Cullingford, C. (1995) British children's attitudes to Germany and the Germans. in Cullingford, C. and H. Husemann (eds.). *Anglo-German attitudes*. Brookfield, Vermont: Ashgate: Avebury, 39–56.

Cuvelier F. (1998) *Verbondenheid. Het ontstaan van menselijke relaties*. Kapellen: Pelckmans.

Czykwin, E. (1999) *Próba modyfikacji stereotypów i uprzedzeń w warunkach szkoły*, in *Edukacja międzykulturowa w wymiarze instytucjonalnym* Nikitorowicz, J., and M. Sobecki (eds). Białystok: Trans Humana.

Dahlberg, G., Moss, P., and Pence, A. (2002) *Från kvalitet till meningsskapande. Postmoderna perspektiv – exemplet förskolan*. Stockholm: HLS Förlag.

Dalli, C. (1999) Starting childcare before three: Narratives of experience from a tri-partite focus (Doctoral theses). University of Wellington, NZ.

Damasio, A. (1994) *O Erro de Descartes: Emocao, razao, e cerebro humano.* (Descartes' Error). Lisboa: Publicacoes Europa-America.

Damasio, A. (1999) *O Sentimento de Si: O corpo, a emocao e aneurobiologia da* consciencia. (The Feeling of what Happens). Lisboa: Publicacoes Europa-America.

Damon, W. (1977) *The social world of the child.* San Francisco CA: Jossey-Bass.

Darling, N., and Steinberg, L. (1993) Parenting style as context: An integrative model. *Psychological Bulletin,* 113(3), 487–496.

Davis, H. A. (2001) The quality and impact of relationships between elementary school students and teachers. *Contemporary Educational Psychology, 26,* 431–453.

Dekker, H. (1999b) *National favoritisme, germanofobie, en Europees burgerschap; Socialisatie van emoties* (National favouritism, Germanophobia, and European citizenship; Socialization of emotions). Utrecht: Utrecht University, AWSB. www.ercomer.org.

Dekker, H. (1994a) Political competence of the younger generation in Western Europe: creating a context for future national and European political socialization research. in R. F. Farnen (ed.). *Nationalism, ethnicity, and identity. Cross national and comparative perspectives.* New Brunswick.

Dekker, H. (1994b) Socialization and education of young people for democratic citizenship. Theory and research. in Edwards, L. and P. Munn, K. Fogelman (eds.). *Education for democratic citizenship in Europe. New challenges for secondary education.* Lisse, NL: Swets and Zeitlinger. 48–90.

Dekker, H. (1991) Political socialization theory and research. in Dekker, H. and R. Meyenberg (eds.). *Politics and the European younger generation. Political socialization in Eastern, Central and Western Europe.* Oldenburg, FRG: BIS. 16–58.

Dekker, H. (1993) European citizenship. How European are young Europeans expected to be and how European are they in fact? In Farnen, R.F. (ed.) (1993). *Reconceptualizing politics, socialization, and education. International perspectives for the 21st century.* Oldenburg: BIS. 519–545.

Dekker, H., and L. B. Jansen (1995) Attitudes and stereotypes of young people in the Netherlands with respect to Germany. in Hübner-Funk, S., and L. Chrisholm, M. du Bois-Reymond, B. Sellin (eds.). *The puzzle of integration. European Yearbook on youth policy and research.* Berlin, New York, NY: De Gruyter. 49–61.

Dekker, H., and M. A. Oostindie (1990) Political socialization effects of an international youth exchange program. in Claussen, B. and H. Mueller (eds.). *Political socialization of the young in East and West.* Frankfurt am Main Lang. 111–132.

Dekker, H., and R. Aspeslagh (1999a) *Ein besonderes Verhältnis; Deutschland und die Niederlande.* (A special relationship; Germany and The Netherlands). Baden-Baden: Nomos.

Dekker, H., R. Aspeslagh, and F. Meijerink (1998) Attitudes toward Germany and other European countries among Dutch youth. *Politics, Groups and the Individual* 7 (1/2), 57–83.

Dekker, H., R. Aspeslagh, M. du Bois, and Reymond (1997). *Duitsland in beeld* (Image of Germany). Lisse: Swets and Zeitlinger.

Dekker, P. (1997) Nationale beeldvorming van Duitsers en Nederlanders in Europees perspectief (National image building of Germans and the Dutch in European perspective). Paper, prepared for presentation at the 1997 conference of the Dutch Political Psychology Association and the Social and Cultural Planning Office.

Delors, J. (1996) Vzgoja in izobraževanje: potrebna utopija (Education: The necessary utopia) in Delors J. et al. Učenje skrit zaklad (Learning: The treasure within). Ljubljana: Ministrstvo za šolstvo in šport.

DeVries, R. (2001) Constructivist education in preschool and elementary school: The sociomoral atmosphere as the first educational goal. In S. L. Golbeck (ed.), Psychological perspectives on early childhood education: Reframing dilemmas in research and practice (pp. 153–180). Mahwah, NJ: Lawrence Erlbaum Associates.

Dijker, A. J. M. (1987) Emotional reactions to ethnic minorities. European Journal of Social Psychology, 17, 305–325.

Dijker, A. J. M. (1991) Cognitive and emotional aspects of stereotypes. Amsterdam: University of Amsterdam.

Dodge, K. A., Pettit, G. S., McClasky, C. L. and Brown, M. M. (1986) Social competence in children. Monographs of the society for Research in Child Development, 51, (2, serial No. 213).

Dortier, J. F. (2001) 'C'était le début du siècle' Sciences Humaines, hors série 34, (September).

Doverborg, E., and Pramling Samuelsson, I. (2000) Att förstå barns tankar. Metodik för barnintervjuer. Stockholm: Liber Utbildningsförlag.

Driscoll, M. P. (1994) Psychology of learning for instruction. Boston MA: Allyn Bacon.

Dubet, F. and Martuccelli, D. (1998) Dans quelle société vivons-nous?, Paris: Le seuil.

Ehrenberg, G. R., Brewer, J. D., Gamoran, A., and Williams, J. D. (2001) Does class size matter? Scientific American, November, 67–69.

Elbaz, F. (1992) Hope, attentiveness, and caring for difference: The moral voice in teaching. Teaching and Teacher Education, 8, 421–432.

Elchardus M., and Smits, W. (2002) Anatomie en oorzaken van het wantrouwen. Brussel: VUB press.

Elschenbroich, D. (1995) Die fruhen Jahre (Early years), Forum Humanwissenschaften. Frankfurter Rundschau, 27. 6., 10.

Enyedi, Z, F. Erös, and Z. Fábián (2001) Authoritarianism and prejudice in present-day Hungary. In Phalet, K. and A. Örkény (eds.). Ethnic minorities and inter-ethnic relations in context. Aldershot: Ashgate, 201–215.

Erikson, E. H. (1959) Identity and the life cycle. New York, NY: Norton.

Erikson, E. (1968) Identity Youth and Crisis. New York, NY: Norton.

Ermenreksdóttir, S. (1951) Jákvæð samskipti nemenda og kennara [Positive interactions between students and teachers]. Menntamál, 24, 64–73.

Erwin, P. (1993) Friendship and peer relations in children. Chichester: John Wiley.

European Commission (1996) *Eurobarometer, Public opinion in the European Union, Report number 46*. Brussels: European Commission, Directorate-General X.

European Commission (2001) *Young Europeans in 2001. Results of a European opinion poll*. Brussels: European Commission, Directorate-General X.

Farnen, R. F. (ed) (1994) *Nationalism, ethnicity, and identity. Cross national and comparative perspectives*. New Brunswick, NJ: Transaction.

Farnen, R. F., H. Dekker, R. Meyenberg, and D. B. German (eds) (1996) (*Democracy, socialization and conflicting loyalties in East and West. Cross-national and comparative perspectives*. New York, NY: St. Martin's Press. London: Macmillan.

Faure, F. and Martinon, C. (1999) 'Les représentations du travail chez les élèves de lycée', *Documents pour l'Enseignement Economique et Social (DEES)* 118, Paris: CNDP.

Ferreira, A. M. (2002) *Desigualdade de Genero no Actual Sistema Educativo Portugues*. Coimbra: Quarteto.

Feys, R. (1998) *Waarden: de moeite waard*. Kortrijk: COV trefdag.

Fize, M. (1990) *La démocratie familiale: évolution des relations parents-adolescents*, Paris: Les Presses de la Renaissance.

Flament, C. (1989) 'Structure et dynamique des représentations sociales', in D. Jodelet, (1989) *Les représentations sociales*, Paris: PUF.

Flanagan, C. A., and Faison, N. (2001) Youth civic development: Implications of research for social policy and programs. *Social Policy Report: A publication of the Society for Research in Child Development, 15,* 3–15.

Flanagan, C. A., Bowes, J., Jonsson, B., Csapo, B., and Sheblanova, E. (1998) Ties that bind: Correlates of male and female adolescents' civic commitments in seven countries. *Journal of Social Issues, 54,* 457–476.

Fontana, D. (ed.) (1994) *The education of the young child*. Oxford: Blackwell.

Foster, V. (1997) Feminist Theory and the Construction of Citizenship Education in Kerry Kennedy (ed) *Citizenship education and the Modern State*. London: Falmer Press.

Foyle, D. C. (1997) Public opinion and foreign policy: elite beliefs as a mediating variable. *International Studies Quaterly*, 41, 141–169.

Friðriksdóttir, K., and Adalbjarnardóttir, S. (2002) 'Ég ákvað að verða kennari þegar ég varð sjö ára' – Lífssaga kennara og uppeldissýn ['I was seven when I decided to become a teacher:'] Teachers' life stories and pedagogical vision. *Uppeldi og menntun* [Journal of Education] 11, 121–146.

Frijda, N. H. (1986) *The emotions*. Cambridge: Cambridge University Press.

Fröbel, F. (1995) *Människans fostran*. (J.-E. Johansson, ed., trans.). Lund: Studentlitteratur.

Gage, N. and Berliner, D. (1998) *Educational Psychology, sixth edition*. Boston MA: Houghton Mifflin.

Gardner, H. (1983) *Frames of mind – The theory of multiple intelligences*. New York, NY: Basic Books.

Gardner, H. (1997) Multiple intelligences as a partner in school improvement. *Educational Leadership, 55*, 1, pp. 20–21.

Gesellschaft für Rationelle Psychologie (1993) *Image der Deutschen im Ausland 1993.* München: Gesellschaft für Rationelle Psychologie. In *Focus*, 9, 1993, 19–22.

Gestettner (1996) *Europe: a children's eye view. A nationwide survey of British school-children's views on Europe.* Northampton: Gestetner. London: The Communication Group plc.

Giddens, A. (2000) Citizenship Education in the Global era, in N. Pearce, and J. Hallgarten *Tomorrow's Citizens: critical debates in citizenship and education.* London: IPPR.

Gilligan, C. (1982) *In a Different Voice: psychological theory and women's development,* London: Harvard University Press.

Giroux, H. (1992) *Border Crossing: Cultural workers and the politics of education.* London: Routledge.

Goetz, T. E., and Dweck, C. S. (1980) Learned helplessness in social situations. *Journal of Personality and Social Psychology,* 39, pp. 246–255.

Goleman, D. (1996) *Emotional Intelligence: why it can matter more than IQ.* London: Bloomsbury.

Good, T .L., and Brophy, J. E. (1997) *Looking in classrooms.* New York, NY: Longman.

Good, T., and Brophy, J. (1995) *Contemporary educational psychology.* New York, NY: Longman.

Gough, H. G., and P. Bradley (1993 Personal attributes of people described by others as intolerant. in Sniderman, P. M., and Ph. E. Tetlock, E. G. Carmines (eds.). *Prejudice, politics, and the American dilemma.* Stanford, CA: Stanford University Press, 60–85.

Hagendoorn, L. (1992) Determinants and dynamics of national stereotypes, in Meyenberg R. and H. Dekker (eds.). *Perceptions of Europe in East and West.* Oldenburg: BIS, 105–122.

Hagendoorn, L. (1993) Ethnic categorization and outgroup exclusion: cultural values and social stereotypes in the construction of ethnic hierarchies. *Ethnic and Racial Studies,* 16, 1, 26–51.

Hagendoorn, L. (1995) Intergroup biases in multiple group systems: the perception of ethnic hierarchies. In Stroebe, W. and M. Hewstone. *European Review of Social Psychology.* Volume 6. London: Wiley, 199–228.

Hagendoorn, L. (2001) Stereotypes of ethnic minorities in the Netherlands. In Phalet, K. and A. Örkény (eds.), *Ethnic minorities and inter-ethnic relations in context,* Aldershot: Ashgate, 43–58.

Hagendoorn, L., and H. Linssen (1994) National characteristics and national stereotypes: a seven-nation comparative study. In Farnen, R. F. (ed.). *Nationalism, ethnicity, and identity. Cross national and comparative perspectives.* New Brunswick, NJ: Transaction, 103–126.

Hagendoorn, L. and J. Hraba (1989) Foreign, different, deviant, seclusive and working class: anchors to an ethnic hierarchy in the Netherlands. *Ethnic and Racial Studies,* 12, 4, 441–468.

Hagendoorn, L., and J. Janssen (1983) *Rechts-omkeer; rechtsextreme opvattingen bij leer-lingen van middelbare scholen.* (Extreme right-wing attitudes among secondary school pupils). Baarn: Ambo.

Hall, C. C. I. (1996) 2001: A race odyssey. in M. P. P. Root (ed), *The multicultural experi-ence: Racial borders as the new frontier.* Thousand Oaks, CA: Sage.

Halldén, G. (2000) Omsorgsbegreppet I förskolan. Olika infallsvinklar på ett begrepp och dess relation till en verksamhet. Inledning, *Rapport från Nätverk för Barnomsorgsforskning*, Göteborg, 20–21 November.

Haug, P. (1998) *Pedagogiskt dilemma: specialundervisning*. Skolverket. Stockholm: Liber AB.

Hayes, N., and Orrell, S. (1993) *Psychology: an introduction*. London: Longman.

Herring, R. D. (1992) Biracial children: An increasing concern for elementary and middle school counselors. *Elementary School Guidance and Counseling, 27(2)*, 123–30.

Hewstone, M. (1986) *Understanding attitudes to the European Community. A social-psychological study in four member states*. Cambridge: Cambridge University Press.

Hewstone, M., and R. Brown (1986) Contact is not enough: an intergroup perspective on the 'contact hypothesis', in Hewstone, M., and R. Brown (eds.). *Contact and conflict in inter-group encounters*. Oxford: Basil Blackwell, 1–44.

Hirschberg, M. S. (1993) The self-perpetuating national self-image: cognitive biases in perceptions of international interventions. *Political Psychology*, 14, 1, 77–98.

Hoffman, M. L. (1980) Moral development in adolescence. in J. Adelson (ed) *Handbook of adolescent psychology*. New York, NY: Wiley, p. 295–343.

Hoffman, M. L. (1988) Moral development. in Bornstein and M. Lamb (eds) *Social, Emotional and Personality. Part 3 of Developmental Psychology: An Advanced Textbook*. London: Erlbaum.

Hofrichter, J. (1993) *Mutual trust between the peoples of EC member states and its evolution 1970 to 1993*. Mannheim: Universität Mannheim, Zentrum für Europäische Umfrage-analysen und Studien.

Hogan, R., and Mankin, D. (1970) Determinants of interpersonal attraction: A clarification. *Psychological Reports*, 26, pp. 235–238.

Hogg, M. A., and Abrams, D. (1988) *Social identification: A social psychology of intergroup relations and group processes*. London: Routledge.

Hooghe M. (2002) Watching television and civic engagement: disentangling the effects of time, programs, and stations, *Harvard International Journal of Press and Politics*, 7, 2, p. 220–240.

Hoover-Dempsey, K. V., and Sandler, H. M. (1997) Why do parents become involved in their children's education? *Review of Educational Research*, 67 (1), 3–42.

Houston, Barbara (1994) 'Should Education be Gender-Free?' in L. Stone (ed), *The Education Feminist Reader*. New York, NY: Routledge.

Hutchings, M., Fülop, M., and Van den dries, A-M. (eds) (2002) *Young People's Economic Understanding of Economic Issues in Europe*. Stoke on Trent, Trentham.

Huyse, L. (1994) *De politiek voorbij, Een blik op de jaren negentig*. Leuven: Kritak.

Illeris, K. (2000) *Lärande i mötet mellan Piaget, Freud och Marx*. Lund: Studentlitteratur.

Inglehart, R. (1991) Trust between nations: primordial ties, societal learning and economic development. In Reif, Karlheinz and Ronald Inglehart (eds) *Eurobarometer. The dynamics of European public opinion. Essays in honour of Jacques-René Rabier*. Basingstoke: Macmillan. 145–185.

Ingvarsdóttir, I. (2003) To take heart in teaching. The nature, use and formation of teacher theories working in the context of the Icelandic secondary school. Unpublished doctoral thesis, University of Reading, England.

INSEE (2002) *Tableaux de l'économie française*, INSEE: Paris.

Jackson, J. W. (1993) Realistic group conflict theory: a review and evaluation of the theoretical and empirical literature. *Psychological Record* 43, 395–414.

Jahoda, G. (1962) Development of Scottish children's ideas and attitudes about other countries. *Journal of Social Psychology*, 58, 91–108.

Jahoda, G. (1963a) The development of children's ideas about country and nationality I. The conceptual framework. *British Journal of Educational Psychology*, 33, 47–60.

Jahoda, G. (1963b) The development of children's ideas about country and nationality II. National symbols and themes. *British Journal of Educational Psychology*, 33, 143–153.

Janowski, A. (1988) Ukryty program polskiej szkoły, *Res Publica*, 4.

Janssens L. (1999) Is personalism still alive in Europe? *Ethical Perspectives*, 6 , 1, p. 55–69.

Jaspars, J. M. F., J. P. van de Geer, H. Tajfel, and N. Johnson (1972) On the development of national attitudes in children. *European Journal of Social Psychology*, 2–4, 347–369.

Jencks, C. (1972) Inequality: *A reassessment of the effect of family and schooling in America*. New York, NY: Basic Books.

Jervis, R. (1976) *Perception and misperception in international politics.* Princeton, NJ: Princeton University Press.

Jodelet, D. (1989) *Les représentations sociales*, Paris: PUF.

Johansson, E. (1999) *Etik i små barns värld. Om värden och normer bland de yngsta barnen i förskolan.* Göteborg: Acta Universitatis Gothoburgensis.

Johansson, E. (2003) *Möten för lärande. Pedagogisk verksamhet för de yngsta barnen i förskolan.* Forskning I focus, nr. 6. Stockholm: Skolverket.

Johansson, E., and Pramling Samuelsson, I. (2002) Förskolans vardag. in Johansson, E. and Pramling Samuelsson, (eds) in *Förskolan – barns första skola.* Lund: Studentlitteratur. p. 9–29.

Johnston, M., and Lubomudrov, C. (1987) Teachers' level of moral reasoning and their understanding of classroom rules and roles. *The Elementary School Journal, 88,* 65–77.

Kagan, J. (1998) A parent's influence is peerless. Harvard education letter research online. http://www.edletter.org/past/issues/1998-nd/parents.shtml (Nov/Dec 1998).

Kao, G. (1995) Asian Americans as model minorities? A look at their academic performance. *American Journal of Education*, 103, 121–159.

Karlsson Lohmander, M., and Pramling Samuelsson, I. (2002) Les cadres pédagogiques de la petite enfance en Europé. Une comparison entre malte, la Norvège, l'Écosse et la Suède. *Politiques d'Éducation et de formation. Analyses et comparaisons internationales. Les politiques éducatives de la petite enfance, 3*(6), 39–55.

Katsillis, J. M. (1987) Education and social selection: A model of high school achievement in Greece. Unpublished doctoral dissertation. Florida State University, Tallahassee, Florida.

Katz, L. (2001) *The right of the child to Develop and Learn in Quality Environments.* Opening address at the OMEP conference, Santiago, Chile, July 31.

Katz, L., and McClellan, D. E. (1997) *Fostering Children's Social Competence: The teacher's role.* NAEYC.

Khawajkiie, E., Muller, A., Niedermayer, S., and Jolis, C. U. (eds) (1996) *What makes a good teacher? Children speak their minds Qu'est-ce qu-un bon maitre? Les enfants ouvrent leur coeur. Como debe ser un buen maestro? Los ninos opinan.* Report no Ed-96/ES/3. Paris, UNESCO.

Kingdom, E. (1996) Gender and Citizenship Rights. in Demain, J. and Entwistle, H. (eds) *Beyond Communitarianism: Citizenship, Politics and Education.* London: MacMillan Press.

Klerfelt, A. (2002) *Var ligger forskningsfronten – 67 avhandlingar i barnpedagogik under två decennier, 1980–1999.* Skolverket. Stockholm: Liber.

Klus-Stańska, D. (2000) *Konstruowanie wiedzy w szkole.* Olsztyn: Wyd.UW-M.

Kohlberg, L. (1984) *Essays on moral development. 2, The psychology of moral development.* San Francisco, CA: Harper and Row.

Kojima, H. (1986) Child Rearing Concepts as a Belief-Value System of the Society and the Individual. In Stevenson, H., H. Azuma, K. Hakuta (eds) *Child Development and Education in Japan.* New York, NY: W. H. Freeman.

Krathwohl, D., Bloom, B., and Masia, B. (1964) *Taxonomy of educational objectives.* Handbook 2, *Affective domain.* New York, NY: McKay.

Krek, J. (ed.) (1996) *White paper on education in the Republic of Slovenia.* Ljubljana: Ministry of Education and Sport.

Kroflič, R. (1997) *Avtoriteta v vzgoji (Authority in education).* Ljubljana: Znanstveno in publicistično središče.

Krzywosz, R. B., Holden, C., Papoulia, T. P., de Freitas, M. L., Verkst, H., Pergar, K. M., Gocsal, A., and Korhonen, R. (2002) Attitudes and identity: a comparative study of the perspectives of European children. in Ross A. (ed) *Future Citizens in Europe.* London: CiCe.

Krzywosz-Rynkiewicz, B., Topczewska, E., and Derkowska, M. (2001) *Tolerancja dzieci wobec odmiennych wyznań i narodowości a doświadczenia szkolne,* in L. Hurło (ed) *Wokół pytań o współczesnego nauczyciela.* Warszawa: WSPTWP.

Ladd, G. W., and Burgess, K. B. (1999) Charting the relationship trajectories of aggressive, withdrawn, and aggressive/withdrawn children during early grade school. *Child Development,* 70, 4, 910–929.

Ladd, G. W. *et al.* (1996) Friendship Quality as a Predictor of Young Children's Early School Adjustment. *Child Development,* 67, 3. pp. 1103–1118.

Laevers F. (1997) Assessing the quality of childcare provision: involvement as criterion. *Researching Early Childhood,* 3, pp. 151–165.

Lambert, W. E. and O. Klineberg (1967) *Children's views of foreign peoples. A cross-national study.* New York, NY: Appleton-Century-Crofts.

Lanoye T. (2002) *Boze tongen.* Antwerpen: Prometheus.

Lautier N., (1997) *La rencontre de l'histoire,* Lille: Septentrion Presses universitaires.

LeDoux, J. (1996) *The emotional brain. The mysterious underpinnings of emotional life.* New York, NY: Simon and Schuster.

LeVine, R. A. and D. T. Campbell (1972) *Ethnocentrism: theories of conflict, ethnic attitudes, and group behavior.* New York, NY: Wiley.

Levy, B. (1996) Improving memory in old age through implicit self-stereotyping. *Journal of Personality and Social Psychology,* 71, 1092–1107.

Lewis, C. C. (1995) *Educating hearts and minds.* New York, NY: Cambridge University Press.

Lewis, R. (2001) Classroom discipline and student responsibility: The students' view. *Teaching and Teacher Education, 17,* 307–319.

Lickona, T. (1991) *Educating for character: How our schools can teach respect and responsibility.* New York, NY: Bantam.

Lindgren, H. C., and Suter, W. N. (1985) *Educational psychology in the classroom.* Pacific Grow, CA: Brooks/Cole Publishing Company.

Linssen, H. (1995) *Nationality stereotypes in Europe: content and change.* Dissertation. Utrecht: ISOR.

Linssen, H., L. Hagendoorn, and L. Matheusen (1996). Changing nationality stereotypes through contact: an experimental test of the contact hypothesis among European youngsters. in Farnen, R. F. *et al.* (eds.) (1996). *Democracy, socialization and conflicting loyalties in East and West.* New York, NY: St. Martin's Press. London: Macmillan. 265–291.

Linville, P. W. (1985) Self complexity and affective extremity: Don't put all of your eggs in one basket. *Social Cognition,* 3, 94–1120.

Linville, P. W. (1987) Self-complexity as a cognitive buffer against stress-related illness and depression. *Journal of Personality and Social Psychology,* 52, 663–676.

Lodewijks-Frencken, E. (1995) *De morele opvoeding van het jonge kind.* Baarn, Nelissen.

Łodziński, S. (1995) *Główne problemy polityki wobec mniejszości narodowych w Polsce w latach 1989–1994,* in *Ludzie i instytucje. Stawanie się ładu społecznego. Pamiętnik IX Ogólnopolskiego Zjazdu Socjologicznego.* Lublin Wyd.UMCS.

Logan R. D. (1986) A reconceptualization of Erikson's theory: repetition of existential and instrumental themes, *Human Development,* 29, 125–136.

Løkken, G. (2000) Using Merleau-Pontyan phenomenology to understand the toddler. Toddler interactions in child day-care, *Nordisk pedagogik, 20,* 1.

Lynch, E., and Hanson, M. (1992) *Developing cross-cultural competence.* Baltimore, MD: Brookes.

Maccoby, E. E. (1992) The role of parents in the socialisation of children: An historical overview. *Developmental Psychology,* 28 (6), 1006–1017.

Mackie, D. M., and D. L. Hamilton (eds.) (1993) *Affect, cognition, and stereotyping: interactive processes in group perception.* San Diego, CA: Academic Press.

Makarovič, J. (1984) *Družbena neenakost, šolanje in talenti (Social inequality, schooling and talents).* Maribor: Založba Obzorja.

Marcus, G. E. (1991) Emotions and politics: hot cognitions and the rediscovery of passion. *Social Science Information*, 30, 195–232.

Markus, H., and R. L. Moreland, J. Smith (1985) Role of the self-concept in the perception of others. *Journal of Personality and Social Psychology*, 6, 49, 1494–1512.

Martin, J. R. (1994) Excluding Women from the Educational Realm in L. Stone (ed) *The Education Feminist reader*. New York, NY: Routledge.

Maslow, A. H. (1954) *Motivation and personality*. New York, NY: Harper and Row.

McCaslin, M., and Good, T. (1996) The informal curriculum. in D. C. Berliner and R. C. Calfee *Handbook of educational psychology*. New York, NY: Macmillan. pp. 622–670.

McFall, R. M. (1982) A review and reformulation of the concept of social skills. *Behavioral Assessment*, 4, pp. 1–33.

McGarty, C., Haslam, S. A., Hutchinson, K. J., and Turner (1994) The effects of salient group memberships on persuasion. *Small Group Research*, 25, 267–293.

McIlveen, R., and Gross, R. (1997) *Developmental psychology*. London: Hodder and Stoughton.

Mejias, J. (1999) 'La relation modernisation/chômage', *Documents pour l'Enseignement Economique et Social (DEES)* 118, Paris: CNDP.

Milharčič, H. M. (2002) Koncepti šolske pravičnosti (The concepts of educational justice) in Pučko, V. C. R. *et al. Zaključno poročilo projekta: Identifikacija kriterijev za vrednotenje pravičnosti v izobraž evanju*. Ljubljana: Pedagoška fakulteta.

Ministry of Education and Science in Sweden (1998a) *Curriculum for pre-school. Lpfö 98*. Stockholm: Fritzes.

Ministry of Education and Science in Sweden (1998b) *Curriculum for the compulsory school, the pre-school class and the after school centre. Lpo 94*. Stockholm: Fritzes.

Misiejuk, A. (1995) *Stereotypy i uprzedzenia w klasie szkolnej, in Edukacja między-kulturowa*. Białystok: Trans Humana.

Misiejuk, A. (1999) '*Ja wobec innego' – program edukacyjny żyjących w przestrzeni wielokulturowej, in* Nikitorowicz, J. and M.Sobecki (eds) *Edukacja międzykulturowa w wymiarze instytucjonalnym*. Białystok: Trans Humana.

Misiejuk, D. (1997) *Edukacja międzykulturowa w opinii nauczycieli – komunikat z badań, in* Kotusiewicz, A., G.Koć-Seniuch and J.Niemiec (eds) *Myśl pedeutologiczna i działanie nauczyciela*. Warszawa-Białystok: Wyd ŻAK.

Molinier, P. (1994) in C. Guimelli, *Structures et transformations des représentations sociales,* Delachaux et Niestlé.

Molloy, M. (1999) Women's studies/Cultural Studies: Pedagogy, Seduction and the Real world. in Michael Peters (ed) *After the Disciplines: The emergence of Cultural Studies*. Westport, Connecticut: Bergin and Garvey.

Moscovici S. (1976, 1st ed. 1961) *La psychanalyse, son image et son public*. Paris: PUF.

Musek, J. (1993) *Osebnost in vrednote (Personality and values)*. Ljubljana: Educy.

Muszyński, H. (1976) *Zarys teorii wychowania*. Warszawa: PWN.

Muxel, A. (1996) *Les jeunes et la politique,* Paris: Hachette.

Newby, M., Rickards, T., and Fisher, D. (2001) *A model of the relationship between teacher and student perceptions of classroom interactions.* Paper presented at the Annual Meeting of the American Educational Research Association, Seattle, WA, April 10–14.

Newcomb, A. F., Bukowski, W. M., and Patee, L. (1993) Children's peer relations: A meta-analytic review of popular, rejected, neglected, controversial, and average sociometric status. *Psychological Bulletin,* 113, 1, pp. 99–128.

Niedermayer. O. (1995) Trust and sense of community. in Niedermayer, O., and R. Sinnott (eds). *Public opinion and internationalized governance.* Beliefs in government; volume two. Oxford: Oxford University Press, pp. 227–245.

Niemi, R. G., and M. A. Hepburn (1995) The rebirth of political socialization. *Perspectives on Political Science,* 24, 1, pp. 7–16.

Niffenegger, J. P., and Willer, L. R. (1998) Friendship Behaviors during Early Childhood and Beyond. *Early Childhood Education Journal,* 26, 2, pp. 95–99.

Nikitorowicz, J. (1997) *Nauczyciel i szkoła w aspekcie edukacji międzykulturowej,* in Kotusiewicz, A., G. Koć-Seniuch, and J. Niemiec (eds) *Myśl pedeutologiczna i działanie nauczyciela.* Warszawa-Białystok: Wyd ŻAK.

Nikitorowicz, J. (1999) *Projektowanie edukacji międzykulturowej w perspektywie demokratyzacji i integracji europejskiej,* in Nikitorowicz, J. and M. Sobecki (eds) *Edukacja międzykulturowa w wymiarze instytucjonalnym.* Białystok: Trans Humana.

Noddings, N. (1999) 'Care, Justice, and Equity' in M.S. Katz. N.Noddings and K.A.Strike (eds) *Justice and Caring: the search for common ground in education,* New York, NY: Teachers College Press.

Nucci, L. (1987) Synthesis of research on moral development. *Educational Leadership,* 44, 5, 86–92.

Okagaki, L., and Frensch, P. A. (1998) Parenting and children's school achievement: A multi-ethnic perspective. *American Educational Research Journal,* 35, 123–144.

Okun, B. F. (1996) Understanding diverse families: What practitioners need to know. New York, NY: Guildford.

Örkény, A., and I. Szabó (2001) Representations of minorities among Hungarian children. in Phalet, K., and A. Örkény (eds.), *Ethnic minorities and inter-ethnic relations in context.* Aldershot: Ashgate, 139–158.

Oser, F. K. (1992) Morality in professional action: A discourse approach for teaching. in F. K. Oser, A. Dick, and J. Patry (eds.), *Effective and responsible teaching. The new synthesis* (pp. 109–125). San Fransisco: Jossey-Bass.

Parke, P. D., and Ladd, G. W. (1992) *Family-peer relationships: Modes of linkages.* Hillsdale, NJ: Erlbaum.

Pateman, C. (1989) *The Disorder of Women: Democracy, Feminism and Political Theory.* Stanford: Stanford University Press.

Pateman, C. (2000) The Patriarchal Welfare State in Kate Nash (ed) *Readings in Contemporary Political Sociology.* Oxford: Blackwell.

Patterson, G. R., DeBaryshe, B., and Ramsey, E. (1993) A developmental perspective on antisocial behavior, in M. Gauvain, and M. Cole (eds.). *Readings on the development of children.* New York, NY: Scientific American Books.

Pavlov, I. (1927) *Conditional reflexes.* Oxford: Oxford University Press.

Percheron, A. (1993) *La socialisation politique,* Paris: Colin.

Pergar, K. M. (1998) Teaching younger children, in Peček, M. Č. (ed.) *European trends in primary school teacher education.* Ljubljana: Pedagoška fakulteta Univerze v Ljubljani.

Pergar, K. M. (1999). Social dimension of early education in Hytonen, J., C. R. Pučko, G. Smyth (eds.) *Teacher education for changing school.* Ljubljana: Pedagoška fakulteta.

Pergar, K. M. (2001) Can the teacher's personality influence development of identity in pupils, in Ross: A. (ed.) *Learning for a democratic Europe.* London: CiCe.

Pergar, K. M. (2002) Pravičnost v izobraževanju in socialno ekonomski status iz perspektive razvojne psihologije (Justice in education and social-economic status in perspective of developmental psychology). V. C. R. Pučko *et al. Zaključno poročilo projekta: Identifikacija kriterijev za vrednotenje pravičnosti v izobraževanju.* Ljubljana: Pedagoška fakulteta.

Persson, P. (2001) *Elevers olikheter och specialpedagogisk kunskap.* Stockholm: Liber AB.

Pettigrew, T. F. (1979) The ultimate attribution error. *Personality and Social Psychology Bulletin,* 5, 461–476.

Pettigrew, T. F. (1986) The intergroup contact hypothesis reconsidered. in Hewstone, M. and R. Brown (eds.). *Contact and conflict in intergroup encounters.* Oxford: Basil Blackwell, 169–195.

Phalet, K., and E. Poppe (1997) Competence and morality dimensions of national and ethnic stereotypes: a study in six Eastern European countries. *European Journal of Social Psychology,* 27, 703–723.

Piaget, J. (1961) *La psychologie de l'intelligence (Psychology of inteligence).* Paris: Libraire Armand Colin.

Piaget, J., and A.-M. Weil (1951) The development in children of the idea of the homeland, and of relations with other countries. *International Social Science Bulletin,* 3, 561–578.

Pianta, R. C., and Steinberg, M. (1992) Teacher-child relationships and the process of adjusting to school. in R. C. Pianta (Ed.), *Beyond the parent: The role of other adults in children's lives* (pp. 61–80). San Francisco, CA: Jossey-Bass.

Pittinsky, T. L., Shih, M., and Ambady, N. (1999) Identity Adaptiveness: Affect Across Multiple Identities. *Journal of Social Issues,* 55(3), 503–518.

Pluchik, R. (1991) Emotions and evolution. *International Review of Studies on Emotions,* 1. pp. 37–58.

Poppe, E. (1999) *National and Ethnic Stereotypes in Central and Eastern Europe; a study among adolescents in six countries.* Amsterdam: Thela-Thesis.

Power, F. C., Higgins, A., and Kohlberg, L. (1989) *Lawrence Kohlberg's approach to moral education.* New York, NY: Columbia University Press.

Powlick, Ph. J. (1995) The sources of public opinion for American foreign policy officials. *International Studies Quarterly,* 39, 427–451.

Pramling Samuelsson, I. (2002a) *The Child's Own Culture in Modern Societ*, invited address at Forum: Theaterarbeit International Symposium: Children's Theatre and Children's Culture, Lingen (Ems), Germany, 16–22 June.

Pramling Samuelsson, I. (2002b) Globalisering i förskola och skola (3–12 år), *Förstudierapport för Sida angående arbete med barn och för barn inom ämnesområdet internationalisering*. Stockholm: Sida.

Pramling Samuelsson, I., and Asplund Carlsson, M. (2003*) Det lekande lärande barnet – I en utvecklingspedagogisk teori*. Stockholm: Liber.

Pučko, R. C. (2002) Poduspešnost (Underachievement) in Pučko, V C. R. *et al. Zaključno poročilo projekta: Identifikacija kriterijev za vrednotenje pravičnosti v izobraževanju*. Ljubljana: Pedagoška fakulteta.

Putkiewicz, E., Wiłkomirska, A., and Zielińska, A. (1997) *Szkoły państwowe a szkoły społeczne. Dwa światy socjalizacji*. Warszawa: Stołeczne Towarzystwo Oświatowe.

Quillian, L. (1995) Prejudice as a response to perceived group threat: Population composition and anti-immigrant and racial prejudice in Europe. *American Sociological Review* 60, 586–611.

Qvarsell, B. (2001) Det problematiska och nödvändiga barnsperspektivet, in Montgomery, H. and Qvarsell, B. (eds) *Perspektiv och förståelse. Att kunna se från olika håll*, pp. 90–105. Stockholm: Carlssons.

Raaijmakers, Q. A. W., W. H. J. Meeus, and W. A. M. Vollebergh (1986) Politieke opvattingen bij LBO- en MAVO- scholieren (Political views among lower vocational and middle general secondary education school students). in Dekker, H. and S. A. Rozemond, Th. J. IJzerman (eds) *Politieke socialisatie* (Political socialization). Culemborg: Educaboek. 83–102.

Robertson, I. (1989) *Society – A Brief Introduction*. New York, NY: Worth Publishers.

Rocher, G. (1970) *Introduction à la sociologie générale*. Paris: Points-Seuil.

Roeser, R. W., Midgley, C., and Urdan, T. C. (1996) Perceptions of school psychological environment and early adolescents' psychological and behavioural functioning in school: The mediating role of goals and belonging. *Journal of Educational Psychology, 88*, 408–422.

Rogoff, B. (1990) *Apprenticeship in thinking: Cognitive development in social context*. Oxford: Oxford University Press.

Roland-Lévy, C. and Ross. A. (eds) (2003) *Political Learning and Citizenship in Europe*. Stoke on Trent: Trentham.

Roopnarine, J. L., and Carter, D. B. (1992) The cultural context of socialisation: A much ignored issue! in I. E. Sigel (series ed) and J. L. Roopnarine and D. B. Carter (eds.), *Annual advances in applied developmental psychology: Vol. 5. Parent-child socialisation in diverse cultures*, 245–251. Norwood, NJ: Ablex.

Rosenberg, S., and G. Wolfsfeld (1977) International conflict and the problem of attribution. *Journal of Conflict Resolution*, 21, 75–103.

Rus, V. (1995) *Slovenija po letu 1995 – razmišljanja o prihodnosti (Slovenia after 1995 – thinking about the future)*. Ljubljana: Fakulteta za družbene vede.

Rutter, M., and Rutter, M. (1992) *Developing Minds. Challenge and Continuity Across the Life Span.* New York, NY: Basic books.

Ryan, R. M., Stiller, J. D., and Lynch, J. H. (1994) Representation of relationships to teachers, parents, and friends as predictors of academic motivation and self-esteem. *Journal of Early Adolescence, 14,* 226–249.

Säfström, C. A. (2002) *Postmodernitet, institutionen för pedagogik,* lecture Växjö Universitet, 16 May.

Säljö, R. (2000) *Lärande i praktiken. Kultur, kommunikation och tänkandets redskap.* Stockholm: Prisma.

Sammon, G. (1996) *Goethe-Institut Survey: 1996 British school-students'image of Germany and the Germans.* London: Goethe Institut.

Schaap J. (1984) *Samen leren leven en geloven. Omgaan met kernwoorden van geloven in dialogisch leren en begeleiden.* Gravenhage: Boekencentrum.

Seixo, C., and Trigo-Santos, F. (2001) 'Genero e Perspectivas de Cidadania', in *Itinerarios: Investigar em educacao,* 1(II), 803–812. Lisboa: CIEFCUL.

Selman, R. L. (1980) *The growth of interpersonal understanding.* New York, NY: Academic Press.

Sherif, M. (1966) *In common predicament. Social psychology of intergroup conflict and cooperation.* Boston, MA: Houghton Mifflin.

Sherif, M. and Sherif, C. W. (1969) *Social psychology.* New York, NY: Harper.

Sherif, M. and Sherif, C. W. (1979) Research on intergroup relations. In Austin, W. G. and Worchel, S. (eds.). *The social psychology of intergroup relations.* Montery, CA: Brooks/Cole. 7–18.

Sherif, M., Harvey, O. J., White, B. J., Hood, W. E., and Sherif, C. W. (1961) *Intergroup conflict and cooperation: The robbers cave experiment.* Norman, OK: University of Oklahoma Press.

Sinnott, R. (1995) Bringing public opinion back in. In Niedermayer, O., and R. Sinnott (eds). *Public opinion and internationalized governance. Beliefs in government* [volume two]. Oxford: Oxford University Press, 18–32.

Sjøberg, S. (2000) *Naturvetenskap som allmänbildning.* Lund: Studentlitteratur.

Skinner, B. (1954) The science of learning and the art of teaching. *Harvard Educational Review,* 24, 2. pp. 86–97.

Skolverket (2000) *Med demokrati som uppdrag.* Stockholm: Liber.

Slavin, R. E. (1994) *A practical guide to cooperative learning.* Boston MA: Allyn and Bacon.

Smith, E. R. (1993) Social identity and social emotions: toward new conceptualizations of prejudice. In Mackie, D. M. and D. L. Hamilton (eds.). *Affect, cognition, and stereotyping: interactive processes in group perception.* San Diego, CA: Academic Press. 297–315.

Smith, F. (1986) *Insult to Intelligence.* New York, NY: Arbor House.

Smith, P. K., Cowie, H. and Blades, M. (1998). *Understanding Children's Development.* Oxford: Blackwell.

Sniderman, P. M., Ph. E. Tetlock, and E. G. Carmines (eds.) (1993) Prejudice and politics: an introduction. In Sniderman, P. M., and Ph. E. Tetlock, E. G. Carmines (eds.). *Prejudice, politics, and the American dilemma*. Stanford, CA: Stanford University Press, 1–31.

Solomon, D., Battistich, V., Watson, M., Schaps, E., and Lewis, C. (2000) A six-district study of educational change: Direct and mediated effects of the Child Development Project. *Social Psychology of Education, 4,* 3–51.

Šolska zakonodaja I (School legislation I) (1996) Ljubljana: Ministrstvo za šolstvo in šport.

Sommer, D. (1997) *Barndomspsykologi. Utveckling i en förändrad värld*. Stockholm: Runa.

SOU (1985) *Förskola-skola. Betänkande av Förskola-skola-kommittén*. Stockholm: Gotab.

Stanulis, R. N., and Manning, B. H. (2002) The teacher's role in creating a postive verbal and nonverbal environment in the early childhood classroom. *Early Childhood Educational Journal, 30,* 3–8.

Stassen, B. K. (1994) *The developing person through the life span*. New York, NY: Worth.

Stevenson, H. W. (1992) Learning from Asian schools. *Scientific American*, 267, 6, 32–40.

Stillwell, R. and C. Spencer (1973) Children's early preferences for other nations and their subsequent acquisition of knowledge about those nations. *European Journal of Social Psychology*, 3, 3, 345–349.

Stroebe, W., A. Lenkert, and K. Jonas (1988) Familiarity may breed contempt: the impact of student exchange on national streotypes and attitudes. in Stroebe, Wolfgang, *et al.* (eds) *The social psychology of intergroup conflict. Theory, research and applications*. Berlin Springer, 167–187.

Tajfel, H. (1970) Experiments in intergroup discrimination. *Scientific American*, 23, 96–102.

Tajfel, H. (1978) Social categorization, social identity and social comparison. in Tajfel, H. (ed.). *Differentiation between social groups. Studies in the social psychology of intergroup relations*. London: Academic Press. 61–76.

Tajfel, H. (1981) *Human groups and social categories*. Cambridge: Cambridge University Press.

Tajfel, H. (1982) *Social identity and intergroup relations*. Cambridge: Cambridge University Press.

Tajfel, H. and J. C. Turner (1986) The social identity theory of intergroup behaviour. In Worchel, S. and W. G. Austin (eds.). *Psychology of intergroup relations*. Chicago, IL: Nelson-Hall.

Tajfel, H., Billig, M. G., Bundy R. P. and Flament, C. I. (1971) Social categorization and intergroup behaviour. *European Journal of Social Psychology*, 1, 149–177.

Tajfel, H., G. Jahoda, C. Nemeth, J. D. Campbell, and N. Johnson (1970) The development of children's preference for their own country. A cross-national study. *International Journal of Psychology*, 5, 4, 245–253.

Teven. J. J., and McCroskey, J. C. (1996) *The relationships of perceived teacher caring with student learning and teacher evaluation*. Paper presented at the Annual Meeting of the Speech Communication Association, San Diego, CA, Nov. 23–26.

Thery, I. (2002) La famille va plutôt bien, *Res publica*, 29, Paris, May.

Thomas, J. A., and Montomery, P. (1998) On becoming a good teacher: Reflective practice with regard to children's voices. *Journal of Teacher Education, 49*, 372–380.

Thorndike, E. (1913) *The psychology of learning: Educational psychology.* New York, NY: Teachers College Press.

Toličič, I., and Zorman, L. (1977) *Okolje in uspešnost učencev.* Ljubljana: Državna založba Slovenije.

Torney-Purta, J., J. Schwille, and J. Amadeo (1999) *Civic education across countries: Twenty-four national case studies from the IEA Civic Education Project.* Amsterdam: The International Association for the Evaluation of Educational Achievement.

Torney-Purta, J., R. Lehmann, H. Oswald, and W. Schulz (2001) *Citizenship and education in twenty-eight countries. Civic knowledge and engagement at age fourteen.* Amsterdam: The International Association for the Evaluation of Educational Achievement.

Trevarthen, C. (1992) The Self Born in Intersubjectivity: The Psychology of Infant Communicating, in U Neisser (ed), *Ecological and Interpersonal Knowledge of the Self.* Cambridge, MA: Cambridge University Press.

Tsouroufli, M. (2002) 'Gender and Teachers' Classroom Practice in a Secondary school in Greece', *Gender and Education*, 14, 2, pp. 135–147.

Turnbaugh-Lockwood, A. (1997) *Conversations with Educational Leaders. Contemporary Viewpoints on Education in America.* New York, NY: State University of New York Press.

Tutiaux-Guillon, N. (2000a) *L'enseignement et la compréhension de l'histoire sociale au collège et au lycée,* Thèse pour le doctorat d'université Paris 7 (1998). Paris: Septentrion thèse.

Tutiaux-Guillon, N., (2000b) *L'Europe entre projet politique et objet scolaire, au collège et au lycée,* Paris: INRP.

Tutiaux-Guillon N. and Mousseau M.-J. (1998) *Les jeunes et l'histoire, identités, mémoires, conscience historique.* Paris: INRP.

UNESCO (1995) *World Education Report.* Oxford: UNESCO Publishing.

United Nations (1989) United Nations Convention on the Rights of the Child. New York, NY: United Nations.

Van Lieshout, C. F. M. (1998) Peer relation and development. in Torsten Husén, T. (eds) *The Education: Complete Encyclopedia.* Oxford: Pergamon/Elsevier.

Vandemaele, M. (2002) *De kracht van je stem.* Brussel: Vlor.

Van Langendonck (1922), Leerkunst: Apperceptie-Interesse, in Decoene, A., and Hovere, Fr. De (eds) *Paedagogische Studiën*, 8, Leuven.

Verkest, H. (2001) Een beeld zegt meer dan duizend woorden, *Basis*, Brussel

Verkest, H. (2002) Vuur brandt alleen op de plaats waar het ook brandt. The clash van 11 september, *Narthex*, 2, 1, pp. 31–35.

Verkest, H. (2003), Hector Defoort: Godsdienstig leven tijdens het Interbellum (1919–1939), in Heus, J. (ed.), *Jaarboek* 2002 (10) Spaenhiers. Koekelare, p. 121–134.

Versteylen, L. (1991) Om te genieten moet je betalen, *Forum,* Leuven: Davidsfonds.

Veugelers, W. (2000) Different ways of teaching values. *Educational Review, 52,* 37–46.

von Wright, M. (2000) *Vad eller vem? En pedagogisk rekonstruktion av G H Meads teori om människors intersubjektivitet.* Göteborg: Daidalos.

Vorauer, J. D., A. J. Hunter, K. J. Main, and S. A. Roy (2000) Meta-stereotype activation: Evidence from indirect measures for specific evaluative concerns experienced by members of dominant groups in intergroup interaction. *Journal of Personality and Social Psychology,* 78, 690–707.

VVKBO (Vlaams Verbond voor het Katholiek Basisonderwijs) (1998) *Leerplan Wereldoriëntatie.* Brussel: Licap.

Vygotsky, L. S. (1978) *Mind and society: The development of higher psychological processes.* Cambridge: Harvard University Press.

Vygotsky, L. S. (1986). *Thought and language.* Cambridge: MIT Press.

Walkerdine, V. (1994) Femininity as Performance. in L. Stone (ed), *The Education Feminist Reader*, New York, NY: Routledge.

Watson, M., Battistich, V., and Solomon, D. (1997) Enhancing students' social and ethical development in schools: An intervention program and its effects. *International Journal of Educational Research, 27,* 571–586.

Weigl, B. (1999) *Stereotypy i uprzedzenia etniczne u dzieci i młodzieży.* Warszawa: Wyd. Instytutu Psychologii PAN.

Weigl, B. and Łukaszewski W. (1992) *Modyfikacja stereotypów i uprzeszeń etnicznych u dzieci,* [in] *Stereotypy i uprzedzenia,* Chlewiński, Z. and Kurcz, I. (eds). Warszawa: Wydawnictwo Instytutu Psychologii PAN.

Weigl, B., and Maliszkiewicz, B. (eds) (1998) *Inni to także my. Program edukacji wielokuturowej w szkole podstawowej.* Gdańsk: GWP

Weinberg, A. 2001 Lien social: crise et recomposition, *Sciences Humaines* HS 34, September.

Wentzel, K. R. (1997) Student motivation in middle school: The role of perceived pedagogical caring. *Journal of Educational Psychology, 89,* 411–419.

Wentzel, K. R. (2002) Are effective teachers like good parents? Teaching styles and student adjustment in early adolescence. *Child Development, 73,* 287–301.

Wentzel, K. R. and Caldwell, K. (1997) Friendships, Peer Acceptance, and Group Membership: Relations to Academic Achievement in Middle School. *Child Development,* 68, 6. pp. 1198–1209.

Wentzel, K. R. and Erdley, C. A. (1993) Strategies for Making Friends: Relations to Social Behavior and Peer Acceptance in Early Adolescence. *Developmental Psychology,* 29, 5. pp. 819–826.

Williams, P. (2001) *Barn lär av varandra. Samlärande i förskola och skola* (Göteborg Studies in Educational Sciences 163). Göteborg: Acta Universitatis Gothoburgensis.

Williams, P., Sheridan, S. and Pramling Samuelsson, I. (2001) *Barns samlärande – en forskningsöversikt* (Skolverkets monografiserie. Stockholm: Fritzes.

Wilterdink, N. (1992) Images of national character in an international organization: five European nations compared. *The Netherlands Journal of Social Sciences* 28 (1), 31–49.

Windisch, U. (1989) 'Représentations sociales, sociologie et socio-linguistique. L'exemple du raisonnement et du parler quotidien', in D. Jodelet, *Les représentations sociales*, Paris: PUF.

Index